Open When

your child struggles at school

you get orders overseas

you're going to your
first military ball

it's

you hit the deployment wall

you love someone
in the military

Letters of Encouragement
for Military Spouses

Lizann Lightfoot

THE SEASONED SPOUSE

Elva Resa ∗ Saint Paul

Open When: Letters of Encouragement for Military Spouses
©2021 by Lizann Lightfoot

The information and advice presented by the author is intended to encourage military families. Each situation is unique, and individuals should seek professional or medical support as appropriate.

Senior editors: Terri Barnes and Hannah Gordon.
Design: Emir Oručević and Andermax Studios.

Scripture quotations marked (NIV) are taken from the *Holy Bible, New International Version*®, NIV®. Copyright © 1973, 1978, 1984, 2011 by Biblica, Inc.™ Used by permission of Zondervan. All rights reserved worldwide. The "NIV" and "New International Version" are trademarks registered in the United States Patent and Trademark Office by Biblica, Inc.™

Library of Congress Cataloging-in-Publication Data

Names: Lightfoot, Lizann, 1982- author.
Title: Open when : letters of encouragement for military spouses / Lizann Lightfoot, the Seasoned Spouse.
Description: Saint Paul : Elva Resa, [2021] | Summary: "This collection of reassuring, informative letters for military spouses offers encouraging words and practical advice about many aspects of military life. Readers choose topics and letters to read when they need guidance tailored to the military life situations they are facing…[on file]"-- Provided by publisher.
Identifiers: LCCN 2021005005 (print) | LCCN 2021005006 (ebook) | ISBN 9781934617595 (paperback) | ISBN 9781934617618 (epub) | ISBN 9781934617625 (kindle edition)
Subjects: LCSH: United States--Armed Forces--Military life. | Families of military personnel--United States--Social conditions--21st century. | Military spouses--United States--Life skills guides. | Lightfoot, Lizann, 1982-
Classification: LCC U766 .L54 2021 (print) | LCC U766 (ebook) | DDC 355.1/20973--dc23
LC record available at https://lccn.loc.gov/2021005005
LC ebook record available at https://lccn.loc.gov/2021005006

1L 2 3 4 5

Elva Resa Publishing
8362 Tamarack Vlg Ste 119-106
St Paul, MN 55125
ElvaResa.com
MilitaryFamilyBooks.com

To Daniel—
Thanks for this military life adventure!

Mail Call

Changes of Address

Sealed With a Kiss

Open When
You Need This Book

Love is powerful, and it will change you. When you love someone in the military, it will change your life: the way you live it, where you live it, and even the way you view the world.

You have opened this book because you love someone who is serving in the military. Maybe you are new to military life. If so, consider this your warm welcome to this community! Perhaps you are dating, engaged, married, or in another type of close relationship with your service member. No matter how you define or describe your relationship now, if you choose to spend your life with a service member, your life will never be the same. There are a few things you will want to know—okay, maybe a few thousand.

Most people begin military life with a lot of confusion, not knowing what questions to ask or where to find answers. I know I did. I love someone in the military too. My husband, Dan, is a member of the United States Marine Corps, and for the past twenty years, I've been participating in military life alongside him. From girlfriend, to fiancée, to wife and mother, I have been by my Marine's side through thick and thin.

If someone tried to tell you everything you need to know about military life all at once it would be overwhelming. The good news is you don't need to know everything all at once. You and your service member will learn from each experience as you go, often with help from friends you make along the way. You will face plenty of challenges together and discover the many rewards of military life. There may be a long journey ahead of you, but you only have to take one step at a time.

From time to time, you will need a word of encouragement, a little light in the dark, a friendly reminder, or simply the reassurance that you are not, in fact, losing your mind. That's why I wrote the letters in this book, to offer encouragement and reassurance that speak to the moments of military life, because I've been there too. I know it helps to hear you're not alone, that your feelings and concerns about military life are quite normal, and that there are good reasons to overcome the negative and focus on the positive.

Each letter from me to you is there ready for you to open when you need it. Perhaps you have written "open when" letters—messages to be saved and read on a certain event or occasion—for a friend or loved one, or someone has written them for you. Open when letters are popular among military couples who expect limited communication during a deployment. They might not have dependable access to email, text messages, or video chats on special occasions or difficult days; so before the deployment, they write a collection of letters, sealed and marked with the day they are to be opened. Some might be for a special day: "Open When It's Your Birthday." Others may meet a particular need: "Open When You're Lonely." Tucked into the service member's luggage or left behind for the spouse at home, each letter offers a loving and personal message when needed most.

That's what this collection of letters is meant to be for you: messages for specific days and challenges in military life from someone who cares and understands. A letter from me to you, to open when you need it. Read a letter when you face a situation that you're not sure about. When you're not sure what to do. Not sure how to feel. Not sure who you can talk to about it.

Each letter stands on its own as an encouraging pep talk or a reassuring hug for a specific situation. Use the Mail Call (table of contents) to find the letter that speaks to what you're going through. You can read the letters one at a time or by section, for example when you're gearing up for a deployment or a big move. Each group of letters begins with a glimpse into my story, a vignette from my own military life journey, so my experiences can help you navigate yours.

No matter what stage of military life you are in right now, this book is for you—in good times and in bad. I hope it will be a source of encouragement and hope, a reminder that you are up to the challenge.

Some days military life may feel like a burden that's too heavy to pick up and carry on your own. Any burden becomes lighter when it is shared, military friend. This book is a reminder that you are part of a caring community of military family members, including me.

These are my letters to you, to offer you hope and confidence on your journey. You are strong. You can do this, and above all, you are not alone—we are in this together!

Love,
Lizann

New to Military Life

My Story
Did I Sign Up for This?

The little wooden tiles on the Marine recruiter's desk said "Education," "Job Security," and "Meaningful Career." The recruiter was arranging the tiles on the desk, talking to my boyfriend, Dan, about all the reasons he should join the United States Marine Corps. I was nineteen years old and had come to the recruiter's office with Dan, but I wasn't included in the conversation. Instead, the recruiter turned on a motivational video for me to watch while he told Dan about all the perks of a military career. The video I watched showed the challenges of Marine Corps basic training, culminating in something called "The Crucible." The film was all about the pride of becoming a Marine.

The video and the recruiter were emphasizing honor, courage, and commitment. But inside, I didn't feel any of that. I felt scared, confused, and overwhelmed. Dan and I had been dating for about a year, and we were discussing marriage. For most of that year, we had been apart. I was in college, and he was a few hours away, working and waiting to be accepted at the local police academy. I had already been wondering whether I was cut out to be a police wife. Then, a clerical error derailed Dan's police academy application, and the next thing I knew we were at the Marine recruiter's office.

The prospect of military life was too much to process or absorb. I didn't have any family members in the military. I had only ever met one military family—a high school friend whose home I had sometimes visited. I didn't know what questions to ask. I had no idea what to expect. I tried to understand Dan's decision and how it would impact me if we got married, but I had no idea what I was getting into.

Even if I had been able to process the possibilities on that summer day in 2001, it wouldn't have mattered. Everything changed with the terrorist attacks on September 11. By then, Dan had signed his papers and was about to go to boot camp. We and the rest of the country were thrown abruptly into a war-time environment. For anyone like me, who loved someone in the military, the effect was life changing.

The next few years were a complete emotional whirlwind for us. While I finished college, my Marine completed boot camp and deployed to Iraq three times in back-to-back combat deployments. We planned to get married, but the military kept throwing obstacles in our way. As the challenges piled on, I didn't have the tools or resources to help me navigate them.

On my college campus, I didn't know anyone else dating someone in the military. I also didn't know much about long-distance relationships, and I knew even less about combat deployments. I felt simultaneously proud of Dan and terrified for his safety. I cried when some people, who viewed me as a representative of the military or the government's military decisions, singled me out to share their political opinions and grievances.

At the same time, I was isolated from the military community. Dan was stationed on the other side of the country and was deployed much of that time, so I rarely spent any time on his base. During those years, I struggled alone, wondering if our relationship would be able to survive military life.

Confusion and bewilderment are common for most of us when we first begin a relationship with a service member or learn our beloved wants to join the military. If you've picked up this book, you have probably choked back some of those feelings. Military life has many giant question marks, and each person will have a different experience.

You probably already know military life involves frequent moves and deployments and time spent apart, but you won't know how any of those feel or how you will handle them until you experience them. Even if you grew up as a military child, your experience as a spouse, spouse-to-be, boyfriend, or girlfriend will be completely different. With military life, as with any life, no one knows exactly what they are getting into until they are in it.

So it's okay if you feel confused or overwhelmed even before you get there. I did too. Yet somehow, despite the challenges, and regardless of my lack of a support network in those early days, my Marine and I found a way forward. We got married after dating for seven years. In more than two decades of military life together, we have experienced plenty of surprises and frustrations. We have always leaned on each other and come back to what we know to be true: we love each other, and our love is strong enough to overcome the challenges.

During those early years, when I often felt alone, I didn't know I was learning the skills to help me survive as a military spouse. I learned independence. I learned how to communicate with Dan across great distances. I learned to define myself by who I am, not by my employment status. And more importantly, I learned the powerful potential within the military community.

After years of feeling isolated in military life and during deployments, I developed a passion to support others who are living this life. Loving someone in the military carved out a piece of my heart, a space that will always be open to other military loved ones. You may feel alone, but no one has to go through military life without help. In these letters, I hope you will find encouragement, hope, and guidance—encouraging words just when you need them most.

As you read, I hope you will remember you are not alone, because we are all in this together.

Open When
Your Lover Is in Basic Training

Dear Military Loved One,

For you and your service member, basic training may be the first time you have been apart. During basic training, recruits or trainees are usually not allowed to leave the training area or have visitors. This means you will not see your loved one until they graduate. Basic military training—also called boot camp, basic combat training, or officer training depending on the service branch and enlisted or officer track—is the initial training phase for your loved one as a new military member. Depending on the service branch, basic training lasts from seven to twelve weeks.

During basic training, communication is limited, even with family. Typically, trainees are not allowed to have personal phones or computers with them. Limited phone calls are allowed on an official phone line, but only at certain times determined by the training schedule, not by personal preference. When you and your loved one are used to being able to call or text whenever you want, the sudden silence can be a huge shock.

Having limited communication with someone you love can feel both frustrating and lonely. In the modern age, where we are used to instant responses, the lack of communication can make you feel both helpless and offended. You may find yourself staring at the phone on weekends, wondering if they will be able to call. When you are feeling invisible, remember that this is a unique time for your relationship to grow. The saying "absence makes the heart grow fonder" is sometimes true. When you spend time apart, you will learn what you miss the most about your love and the little ways they brighten your day. You will also have time to focus on yourself. Spend time with friends and family and nurture healthy relationships with classmates or coworkers. Pursue a hobby or creative project you previously didn't have time to try. During basic training, you are dipping your toe into the confusing waters of military life. This is a good time to test those waters. As you learn the challenges, you will start to form your own coping strategies and support network.

When your loved one arrives at the training location, which will be on a military installation, they may be granted one quick call to check in and tell you their mailing address. Be ready to write it down! It may be a few weeks before you receive the next phone call or even a letter from your loved one, but you can begin sending cards or letters right away. Different branches have different rules about what you are allowed to send trainees during basic training. Be sure to check and follow the regulations for your loved one's unit. Some allow only flat letters or envelopes with no additional food or comfort items. Others allow care packages with snacks, first aid supplies, and photos. Disregarding these rules will only cause your loved one embarrassment or trouble. You may have a personality that does not mind being singled out for attention, but in basic training attention is usually not a positive thing, personally or professionally. This time of intense training is the beginning of your loved one's career, so it's important to follow any regulations or guidelines in place.

In every service branch, this initial training period is demanding and challenging both physically and mentally. Your loved one will experience a structured schedule of strenuous physical training, field exercises, and classroom time. Personal time—even for sleeping—will be limited. The purpose of this intense training period is to develop a sense of mission and team unity. In the end, your loved one will have every right to be extremely proud of their accomplishments.

Because of the physical and mental demands already on your loved one, keep your letters and any communication encouraging and upbeat. Remind them of your love and confidence in them. Reassure them that you want them to do their best. If you can't think of anything else to write, share a poem or the lyrics of a favorite song. The more mail you send, the more encouragement they will receive. Especially when communication is limited, every recruit looks forward to mail call. Even a brief note is much appreciated.

You may wonder whether it is okay to be honest with your service member about how lonely you are and how much you miss them. The answer depends a little on the type of relationship you have and how serious it is. Of course, you will miss them, and it's perfectly acceptable to say so. Let your loved one know how much you look forward to seeing them again. They undoubtedly feel the same way. At the same time, realize they need to stay focused on training and not be too distracted by your relationship or other life events. While it's important to be honest and to answer direct questions, avoid complaining about your loneliness or anything going wrong during this period, such as car repairs or minor illnesses. During basic training, your service member won't have the ability to help you through these challenges and will feel more stressed because they are not able to help you. Whenever possible, it is best to handle these situations on your own or with help from family or friends. You may wish to let your service member know after the fact that there was a problem, and you were able to handle it. This will be much less distracting to them than sending a long letter about family drama and financial concerns. When you are feeling confused or frightened, try to be strong and supportive for your recruit. When they come home, you can catch them up on all the details. In the meantime, find a friend or family member you can lean on and vent to on bad days.

Another source of help and support are websites and online groups where you can connect with other family members whose loved ones are going through military training at the same time. This may be your first introduction to the military community. It's so refreshing to meet other military loved ones and families who can relate to your experiences and answer your questions! There may be an official website or social media channels dedicated to your loved one's training group where the military will announce updates, news, and possibly post photos of the trainees. These are great resources, offering opportunities to learn more about what lies ahead for each of you. This may also be your first introduction to the military community. Reach out and make connections with loved ones and family members of other recruits and candidates, if possible.

When basic training is complete, a graduation ceremony marks the accomplishments of the training class. This is a big event where families are invited to attend and celebrate with their new service member. Many branches incorporate a family day, where you may be invited to visit the training location and see your loved one, either before or after the graduation ceremony. Be sure to communicate with your service member's family to see if they have official graduation information and to coordinate travel plans.

Graduation day is so exciting! But it can also feel confusing visiting a military base and dealing with military rules for the first time. Feel free to ask questions, but also trust the leadership to tell your service member the basic details about family visitors. Planning ahead is essential if you would like to attend your loved one's graduation. You will need a visitor's pass to get on the military installation where the graduation takes place. Find out in advance what identification or paperwork is required to obtain a pass. Passes are generally issued at a visitor's center at the entrance gate of the installation. Nearby hotels are often in demand during graduation, so if you will need a place to stay, make arrangements as early as possible.

After graduation, when your service member returns home, expect them to go through an adjustment period. For weeks, they have been surrounded by a group and have followed strict rules. It will take time for them to readjust to regular life. Typically, service members prepare to leave for their next level of training very soon if not immediately after graduation. If your service member seems distracted or preoccupied after basic training and graduation, be patient. It doesn't mean their feelings for you have changed. They are processing a whole new way of life and a new career. With some understanding and patience, you will both get through it. The more you research, ask questions, and reach out to other military family members, the more reassured you will feel about the challenges ahead of you.

For now, celebrate this milestone! You both made it through basic training and are headed for the next step in the journey!

Open When
You're Dating Long Distance

Dear Lonely One,

There are days when it hurts so much to be away from the one you love. The painful ache never quite leaves your chest. You would do anything just to hear the voice you love. You feel the sting of jealousy when other couples you know are able to call and text each other anytime they like. You know the struggle of saving up gas money for a trip to see your loved one or searching for cheap airfares, all while trying to pay your bills and make ends meet. There are nights you may cry yourself to sleep, longing for the day you can be with your loved one again. Sometimes it feels as if your whole life is just a countdown until the next time you can see each other.

When you are dating long distance, especially when you love someone in the military, it's often difficult to find supportive friends who understand your situation. You probably are frustrated when others question your relationship.

Why are you doing this?

How can they expect you to wait so long?

Are you sure this is the right relationship for you?

Yes, you are sure. You know your love is true. Right now, it is just being tested by time and distance.

My friend, you are surviving a challenge many people would not undertake, and this stage is only temporary. Deep down, you know you'll have the rest of your lives to enjoy each other. That's how you can be certain you will get through this long-distance stage. You can do it the same way military couples have been managing for generations.

Thankfully, long-distance relationships have come a long way in the modern age, thanks to increased communication options. Use whatever technology you have to stay connected, and create regular ways to connect, whether a video chat over a meal or a morning text or email just to say "I love you." Creating rituals will strengthen your relationship and help you both feel loved across the miles. Your relationship doesn't need to stand still when you are apart. It can continue to grow and develop.

Don't forget the old ways of communicating. Write letters often. Emails and text messages are great, but letters have a special place in human connection. The process of writing by hand allows you to pour out your heart and get to the very core of your emotions. You will learn a lot about each other through writing letters and by reading them. You will also have them as a treasure for years to come. Save them, and make sure your loved one does too. Whether you keep them in a box on the top shelf of your closet or display them, tied with a ribbon in a shadow box, the letters you write are precious. They tell the beginning of your love story, and you won't want to lose them.

Begin now to think creatively about ways to celebrate birthdays and holidays when you are not together. In your military life together, you may have to spend many special days apart, but you can still find ways to connect. Find a way to let your loved one know you are thinking about them on any special occasion. Mail a care package, order a unique gift, create something sentimental, or plan a surprise visit. Love prevails, even over great distances.

This is also an important time to cultivate independence. Fill your life with positive people, activities, and work you enjoy, so you don't dwell on the negatives of spending time apart. Even if your relationship comes first in your life, it shouldn't be the only thing that is important to you. Invest time in yourself, so you are always bringing fresh energy to the relationship.

No one gets through military life by themselves. Find support from others. Your military relationship is like a climbing rose bush in a garden. It is growing and blooming into something wonderful, but it needs a supportive trellis or a stable wall to climb. You can build those anchor points as your relationship grows. There will be rough days, times when you are confused, and weeks where you question if you can do this anymore. That's when you need support, whether it is from other military-connected friends or from civilian friends. Lean on them the way a growing flower winds itself around the graceful arch of a lattice wall. Ignore those who say, "You knew what you signed up for." Instead, seek out those amazing friends who have your back in tough times, who will take you out for coffee, bring you dinner, call to check on you. Be there for them on their rough days too.

When possible, take advantage of opportunities to spend time together with your service member as well as your other close friends. Sometimes that may mean you drive a long way to see them for only a few hours. Or you might fly across the country for a weekend visit. Investing in your future together is worth it!

The distance between you is painful right now, but you can do this! When you are celebrating your second, tenth, or even your fiftieth anniversary together, you will look back at these years with a smile, knowing how this difficult time made you grow stronger in your love for each other.

Even now, you are stronger than you know. Just like that sturdy climbing vine, hang in there!

Open When
Others Don't Understand
Military Life

Dear Misunderstood Friend,

Sometimes, loving a service member feels like a lonely place. Military life is a unique world, encompassing only a small fraction of the population, so it's no surprise when others don't understand your relationship with your military loved one. Unfortunately, this means friends and even family members might say unkind words.

Some of their comments may question the value of your relationship or your judgment:

I don't understand how you can be with someone who spends so much time away from you. Are you sure they really love you?

They don't seem to be putting the same effort into the relationship as you are. When are you two going to break up?

I don't think you should marry someone who will never be around and able to spend time with their children.

Other comments serve to awaken your worst fears:

Are you sure they are being faithful to you? I hear a lot of military people cheat.

Aren't you afraid they are going to die?

Other stock phrases show a complete lack of understanding about military life:

Why can't they visit you for your birthday or the holidays? Doesn't the military ever give them a break?

I guess you miss your service member. I can totally relate. My boyfriend went to a weekend conference once, and I was lonely too!

Well, I'm sorry you're going through a difficult time, but you knew what you signed up for when you started dating someone in the military!

Words like these can really sting, especially coming from those you love and care about. People who love you will say hurtful things, not because they want to hurt you but because they don't understand military life. Their thoughtless comments may even cause you to wonder if you are making the right choices. It's so difficult to know what the future holds in any life, but sometimes military life seems to magnify the uncertainty.

You may not have planned to fall in love with someone in the military. Maybe you fell in love with your person before they ever thought about joining the military. Love happens. And even if you fell in love with someone who was already active duty and you knew some of the struggles of military life, the challenges are still there. Be encouraged. When you love someone in the military, you find ways to make it work, even when it's difficult or painful. Even when no one around you understands.

When someone makes an insensitive comment, you can choose how to respond. Take a deep breath and try not to speak in anger to avoid saying something you will regret later. If you can, smile and shrug it off for the moment. If you can't, you're not obligated to offer an answer at all. Change the subject or end the conversation. Either way, don't allow the person or the words to pull you down. It is almost impossible to explain military life to someone who has never experienced it, so don't waste your time and emotional energy on arguments or debate.

If a friend or family member says something insensitive, assume they mean well and are trying to express concern for you. If people you interact with regularly make rude or insensitive comments over and over, tell them their questions and judgments are hurtful. Sometimes people just need to take a step back and see the true impact or weight of their words. If possible, remind them kindly and gently. If they continue to frustrate you, then give the relationship space for a while if possible. You don't have to make room for negative people in your life.

Instead, look for people who are positive, loving, and supportive. Sometimes you will find kindred spirits among other military loved ones, because they understand more of what you are going through. The military community is full of incredibly warm and welcoming people who will be happy to answer questions, let you vent, or sympathize with your frustrating experience. The community of military spouses and significant others also has its fair share of cattiness and drama, but don't let a bad experience scare you away. Keep looking and reaching out to find the people who are understanding and supportive. Reach out to groups in person or online, and you can make great new friends!

When you meet others in military life, you will discover almost everyone goes through this. You aren't alone! Your rude coworker or interfering aunt are not the only annoying or insensitive people in the world. Everyone occasionally deals with frustrating comments from their own friends and family. Learning to handle the comments with calmness and grace will go a long way. Then go to your supportive network. They will all sympathize because they know exactly how you feel and what you are going through!

Open When

You Want to Get Married

Dear Future Military Spouse,

Wow, it's really happening: After the time you have spent dating and getting to know each other, you are preparing to take the next step. You are thinking about marrying into the military! When you dream of your future together, you are excited and giddy. But you probably also have a lot of questions, and you may wonder if you have what it takes to handle a military marriage.

Marriage is a life-changing decision, one you need to make for all the right reasons. While advice from friends or parents can be helpful, ultimately it is your life, your future, and a decision you and your spouse-to-be must agree to together.

If you are questioning whether the time is right for you and your service member to get married, you probably don't doubt your love, but you may have reasonable questions in your mind:

Am I ready to move away from family?

Can I adjust to a new place, find a new job, and make new friends?

Am I ready for the challenges of military life?

Will we have enough money?

If questions like these are burdening you, they are worth exploring. Be assured that no one has all the answers before they get married. Marriage is a huge step for anyone. You and your service member want to do all you can to build a strong foundation for your future, so you should take some time to evaluate the challenges and develop good life skills before you jump into the challenges of military marriage.

Before marriage, it's important to become a strong person on your own. Pursue your interests and education, and make friends. Your military loved one should not be your only friend or the entire focus of your life. You should also have other supportive friendships and personal goals in your own life, apart from your lover. When you follow your loved one without an awareness of your individuality, you risk losing yourself and blaming your loved one for your disappointment.

Given the uncertainties of military life, young military couples often want to get married sooner rather than later. When you are ready to get married, no matter how old or young you are, it helps to examine the challenges military life presents. The more you know, the better you can prepare to meet those challenges.

Before you get married, it's important to develop skills for caring for yourself as an adult. This is true for men and women and includes skills such as planning and preparing meals, driving a car, and managing your money. In military life, you will often be apart from your loved one, even after marriage. You will need to be able to feed yourself healthy, nourishing meals, drive yourself to and from work and appointments, pay bills, and take care of financial decisions.

Learning to live within a budget—spending less than you make— is an essential life skill no matter who you are, married or single, military or civilian. Financial arguments are among the biggest issues in any marriage. Know the financial facts of your future budget and start saving before you get married.

Along those same lines, it will help if you get a degree or job training before marriage. Marketable skills prepare you for a stronger future together. The more skilled you are, the better your job opportunities. Finding a job each time the military moves you will be difficult enough. Not having a degree, professional certification, or job experience further limits your options.

It's tempting to quit school and move to be where your future spouse is stationed right now, but believe me, finishing school is easier now than it will be after you are married. In the future, frequent military moves, deployments, and babies can delay your education. Investing time and establishing job skills before marriage is really an investment in yourself. It will open more opportunities for you and your family and bring you more confidence and satisfaction in the years to come.

As you are preparing for marriage, learn all you can about military life. Do some research. There are many practical benefits in military life as a married couple, including additional pay and housing, healthcare coverage, separation pay during deployment, and connection to a supportive community. None of these on their own are reasons to get married, so don't let these benefits be the deciding reason for marriage. Explore all the facets of military life and know what it will require of you as well as how it will benefit you.

Some of the difficulties military couples face include financial struggles, time apart during deployment, and separation from the support network of extended family. Additionally, many military spouses find it difficult to get a job or maintain a career because of frequent moves. Talk to military spouses and get their perspectives. Ask them to tell you the best and worst. You will hear some difficult stories and some wonderful ones. Talk to as many spouses as you can to get different viewpoints and as complete a picture as possible of military life.

It's so exciting to be engaged, and so hard to wait to begin your life together, but many young military couples struggle because they weren't really prepared for the challenges of adulthood and military life when they got married.

You may think being in love doesn't require thought and planning, but building a life together certainly does. You have nothing to lose and a lot to gain by taking time to determine the right time for marriage. If you feel like people are judging you for wanting to get married sooner rather than later, consider that they might be trying to help you. They want you to succeed and have a happy military marriage. When you make the right choices for yourself and your future, your relationship will have a strong foundation and an even stronger future.

Open When
You're Planning a Military Wedding

Dear Bride or Groom,

Congratulations on your engagement to a service member! You have probably already been discussing options and ideas for your wedding. Maybe you are already finding it challenging to set a date. Your service member is at the mercy of their unit's timeline, so they may not be able to request time off to get married and go on a honeymoon. They may know about an opportunity to take time off—in the military time off is called "leave"—but they may not be able to predict available leave time six months or a year in advance. If you are planning a military wedding, you are about to learn the first rule of becoming a military spouse: be flexible.

Military couples sometimes find themselves rushing to tie the knot before a deployment, from different time zones, in a location where neither of them has family nearby—or all of the above. It's not an easy entry into military life, but it can be done.

Many military couples coordinating a wedding amid a deployment or a move solve some of the difficulties with paperwork by getting officially married ahead of time—either by a minister or justice of the peace—and having the wedding ceremony at a later date. This is especially common if the active-duty member is about to be deployed or transferred overseas. With a marriage certificate entered into military records, your service member is eligible for separation pay and family housing, and you, as a spouse, are eligible for military health insurance and spousal hiring preferences in some jobs. A courthouse wedding is as valid as any fancy nuptials, and maybe that's all you want or need. If you dream of a bigger reception and a traditional celebration with family and friends, you can always plan a big event later.

When deciding on a date for a wedding, consider a national holiday like Memorial Day or Labor Day. Service members may be more likely to have three- or four-day weekends for those holidays—unless they are deployed or training or on other duty. Traveling on a holiday weekend may be inconvenient for your family and guests, but it's one way to improve the odds that your service member will be available for the wedding date. And it makes it more likely they will have time off each year for your anniversary—unless they are deployed, of course.

Often, service members can't get enough consecutive leave for a wedding and a honeymoon in the same month. If this is your situation, consider taking your honeymoon trip a few months later or on your first anniversary. You could have your wedding before a deployment and plan a honeymoon after your spouse returns. Service members accumulate new leave days each month. Separating the events allows time to accrue a few more leave days. It's also a good way to break up the financial costs of the wedding and honeymoon.

Get wedding insurance to help you recover some of your costs in case you have to reschedule. No timeline is ever certain in the military, even leave time to get married, and this is no joke when you are planning a wedding. Deployments can be extended, orders can change to a different location, and natural disasters can require your service member to report for duty even when their leave was previously scheduled and approved. Communicate with your vendors about their cancellation policy due to military requirements. They may offer a military discount or have a special clause to include in the contract. The same goes for your honeymoon plans. I highly recommend travel insurance.

It is certainly a lot to juggle! Working on wedding plans together can be challenging if you are apart before the wedding. If your communication is limited during the planning process, find creative ways to include your spouse-to-be. If there is a decision that doesn't need to be made for a few weeks, provide your loved one with the options and wait for a response. If your officiant wants you to complete a marriage questionnaire, get two copies so you can each read and study separately and discuss it together by phone or video chat. If your loved one is deployed, send care packages with samples of wedding colors, pictures, and decorations. Whenever possible, try to let them handle communications with their own family members, if that helps avoid family drama.

Another decision is whether or not to include military traditions or dress in your wedding ceremony. These are completely optional and should be discussed with your service member. Some want to wear a military uniform, while others feel it is uncomfortable or inconvenient. If you prefer not to include any military traditions or garb in your ceremony, you can still do a military uniform photo shoot before or after you are married.

If you want to include military traditions on your wedding day, your service member has the option to wear a military dress uniform instead of traditional wedding clothing. If service members are invited to be part of the wedding party, it is up to the bride and groom whether their attendants wear a uniform or not. For a military wedding, guests who are in the military may also be invited to come in uniform. Invitations should communicate which uniform is preferred, since there are various types.

Other military traditions for weddings include getting married in a military chapel, having a military chaplain officiate, an arch of swords, sabers, or rifles, using a military sword or saber to cut the cake, and incorporating service branch songs or hymns. Military ceremonies are performed by military members and should follow the requirements of military protocol. You or your service member will need to coordinate first with your military unit or chapel staff about including any military customs in your wedding. Be sure to ask about any policies at your wedding venue before planning anything involving weapons, even ceremonial ones.

Planning a wedding to a military member isn't easy, but it will be worth it. The wonderful thing is there is no right or wrong way to celebrate the beginning of your new life together. Whether you plan a big wedding or a small one, a military ceremony or civilian, whether you invite family or elope to the courthouse, you will be in good company in the military spouse community. Welcome to the family!

Open When
You Become a "Dependent"

Dear New Dependent,

When you became a military spouse, no matter your age, your financial situation, or professional status, you became a military dependent. Don't be alarmed. Being called a dependent is not a value judgment. It's simply a term the military uses to describe a family member—usually a spouse or a child—who is eligible for military support and benefits through their relationship to a service member.

This new description of you as a "dependent" may sound like an insult to you, especially if you are an independent adult with a life and a career of your own.

However, the facts of military life are very mission-oriented, and everything about your new spouse's career is directed to the mission. No matter who you are or what you do, you are less essential to actively completing the mission than your service member. Notice, I didn't say "nonessential," just less essential in the eyes of the military. The military in general recognizes more now than ever how important military spouses are to the wellbeing of the services, but for the purposes of paperwork, you are a dependent.

Your identity as a military dependent is established when your service member enrolls you in the Defense Enrollment Eligibility Reporting System (DEERS) and you receive your military identification (ID) card. Your ID card allows you access to military installations and to your basic benefits, such as medical care and shopping at the exchange or commissary. It also serves as your insurance card for any civilian medical care you receive through the military insurance program. As a military spouse, you should always carry your ID card and keep it secure, just as you do your driver's license or a credit card. It is your passport to military life.

For many of the activities of day-to-day military life, as long as you have a valid ID card, your spouse does not have to be with you. Most official paperwork in military life, however, has to be authorized by the service member, either in person or via power of attorney. When your spouse is deployed or not present for other reasons, a power of attorney will enable you to execute most necessary paperwork.

When you become a military dependent, your spouse's social security becomes the magic number for just about everything. Most of the time, when you are asked for a social security number in a military setting, the answer is your spouse's social security. Very often, you only have to supply the last four digits, and you will soon respond automatically to the two-word request, "Last four?" Trust me, you will hear it often from now on.

Spouses handle the adjustment to dependent status in different ways. Some choose to ignore military connections as much as possible and continue to work, go to school, and live their lives as usual. Others are offended by being called a dependent and may react by separating themselves from the military community or associations. Still others connect deeply to their spouse's military career and rank and re-form their identity to the service member.

Any extreme reaction can be unhealthy for your life and marriage. It is not healthy to completely ignore what your service member does, or to resent the benefits of military life, since these factors will affect you in many ways. But it is also unwise to lose yourself and your self-esteem by focusing only on your spouse's identity.

The adjustment to military life can be difficult, especially if as a new spouse you were used to being employed and truly independent and suddenly find yourself at a new location without a job and dependent on your service member. The best way to look at being a dependent is to focus on the positive benefits, and I don't just mean the healthcare. Being a military spouse or dependent doesn't define you, but it does offer you a connection to a strong and supportive community like no other. Remember, the main reason you are a military spouse is because of the person you love and married.

You may encounter those who disrespect you for your dependent status or how you choose to embrace it. When you are the target of hurtful words, shake it off. What matters is not how others view your choices, but how you view them and how you live them out.

The struggle of being a military dependent and yet an independent person is something you will work out with your service member. It's possible your experience will change at different locations or during different phases of your life. You may have a busy career and social life at one assignment. At another you may be the parent who stays home with small children and gets to know other stay-at-home parents in the neighborhood. At another place, you may experience a period of isolation, but if you realize it is temporary, you can get through it. Don't let temporary circumstances define who you are or how you see yourself.

No matter how you react to becoming a military dependent, and no matter what seasons of life you experience, here's what I want you to hear: you are an individual with unique skills and abilities. You are not inferior to your spouse in any way, no matter how the military defines your status. You are not your service member, and their job should not limit your dreams. Never forget who you are and what your strengths are. Even if your goals have to take a back burner sometimes during a particular move or deployment, don't let them vanish forever. Never forget your service member married you and depends on your love, your support, your thoughts, and your many strengths. Each of you is dependent on the other!

Open When

You Visit a Military Installation the First Time

Dear Visitor,

A military installation feels like a whole new world as soon as you pass through the front gate. But first you have to get through the gate. Your first visit may be when you attend a family day ceremony to meet your service member after basic training or one of their training classes. Or it could be when your military boyfriend or girlfriend invites you to visit. Or maybe your first visit is after you are married to your service member. No matter when you first visit, it helps to have an idea of what to expect.

Whatever the installation is called—post, base, camp, station, or fort—you will have to pass through a security gate to get there. Getting through the gate may feel intimidating, since there are armed guards, warning signs, and a variety of vehicle barriers. Most installations have two or more gates, each guarded by military police or contract security personnel. The main entrance is often called the front gate. To enter any gate, whether walking or driving, you must stop and present a valid military ID card, either active duty or dependent, to the guard on duty. Anyone without a military ID will have to obtain a visitor's pass, which requires a sponsor with valid military ID. There are sometimes exceptions to this rule for large events, when groups are granted access to attend. Still, advance notice is usually required, and visitors will be required to present official photo identification such as a driver's license or passport. If you are going on a military installation as a visitor, check the policy in advance to get details specific to the location and the event, so you don't get held up at the gate. Changes in security conditions also change accessibility to a military installation. Sometimes visitors will not be allowed to enter, and sometimes vehicles will be stopped and searched.

The guards at the gate, whether civilian or military, take their duty to defend the installation seriously and are authorized to use deadly force. Always follow their directions. Showing an ID is always required, and comments about weapons, bombs, or entering unlawfully are taken very seriously. No joking about those topics. Period.

Once you're on the installation, there are some rules you are expected to follow. You will not be able to talk on a cellphone while driving. Speed limits may be lower than in civilian areas, and they are also more rigorously enforced. Pay close attention to all traffic signs. Facilities also may have a dress code, usually posted at the building entrances. Generally, flip flops, revealing clothing, workout attire, and baseball hats should not be worn inside. These requirements vary for different branches, and some locations enforce the rules more than others. It's best to know the expectations and dress accordingly.

During your visit, you may experience a flag ceremony. On US installations around the world, the American flag is raised each morning at a ceremony called reveille and taken down during a ceremony called retreat. For either ceremony, if you are outside and hear the distinctive bugle sounding, you should stop walking and face the flag. If you can't see the flag, notice where others around you are facing and turn that way. If you are driving, traffic may stop for a moment, and you should do the same if you can safely do so. You may see some service members getting out of their vehicles, but this is usually considered optional and certainly subject to safety considerations. During colors, the National Anthem is often played, and you should stand respectfully. During both ceremonies, military members in uniform must salute until the music ends and the flag is no longer in motion. Civilians may choose to place their hand over their hearts and should also stand respectfully until the ceremony is over.

Another place where flag etiquette comes uniquely into play on military installations is at the movie theater. Before the film begins, the National Anthem will be played, accompanied by a patriotic video. All audience members, whether military or civilian, should stand and observe proper courtesy to the flag.

In some ways, a military installation is like a small town, with stores, offices, housing, and other amenities, such as a gym, theater, and library, to support military members and their families. You may hear your service member use some unfamiliar lingo when referring to these facilities, such as commissary, exchange, or MWR.

The commissary is a grocery store. Depending on where you live, items at the commissary are often cheaper than civilian grocery stores. Shoppers at the commissary are required to show a military ID to make purchases. Also good to know: The people who bag groceries at the commissary work for tips only. They will carry your groceries and put them in your car, and it's customary and expected to give them a tip, since they are not paid by the commissary. Ask your military member or a military friend about the going rate for tipping baggers.

An exchange is another kind of store. It is called by various names, depending on the service branch. Smaller exchanges are like convenience stores. Larger ones are more like department stores, where you'll find home goods, furniture, decor, clothing, shoes, books, toys, stationery, even appliances. Like the commissary, a military ID is required to make purchases. No tipping is required or expected at exchanges.

The family support center offers free classes to help you before, during, or after deployments, as well as help making a budget, writing a resume, raising children, and more.

Morale, Welfare, and Recreation (MWR) offers trips, competitions, sports events, and other family activities. They sometimes host concerts or other events for the military community.

Information, Tickets, and Tours (ITT) offers tickets to local attractions and events at a discounted rate for military members and families. If you are going to any show or amusement park, you can save money by getting tickets through them.

Military chapels offer religious support and services of all kinds, and they welcome visitors. The work of military chaplains is to ensure the First Amendment rights of freedom of religion to all military members and their families. Chaplains come from various faiths and denominations and are available to help military members, spouses, and families of all religious beliefs or no religious beliefs. Chaplains are also available to offer advice and counsel with complete confidentiality. You or your service member can talk to them about all kinds of topics, such as marriage and divorce, anxiety, mental health, or abuse. Chaplains can offer help and referrals for many issues.

Most installations also have a military treatment facility, which provides medical services to military members and families. Clinics are most common, where military members and families go for urgent care, routine appointments, immunizations, and other services. Larger installations may also have military hospitals for treatment requiring in-patient care and emergency services. Military members and families are also eligible for insurance through the designated national military healthcare provider, which provides coverage for care received from civilian providers or facilities.

When leaving a military installation, you will not usually have to stop at the gate, unless security measures are in place for an emergency or training. Keep an eye out when approaching the gate and obey any signs or directions from security personnel.

Military installations can feel like a different world, and in many ways they are. Your first visit to a base or post may seem strange, even intimidating, but you will learn to navigate it and the services it provides. It will become more and more familiar as time goes by, and soon almost every installation you visit will feel like home as soon as you enter the front gate.

Open When
It Feels Like You Have No Friends

Dear Lonely Military Friend,

Military life can be downright lonely. Your service member will spend many nights away from home for training missions, schools, temporary duty (TDY) assignments, deployments, and sometimes for regular duty. Moving to a new place where you don't know anyone is intimidating and exhausting.

If you are feeling this way, take heart. Every military spouse sometimes feels alone. We all have times when we are the new spouse on the block or in the unit, and it takes time to build up your new network of friendship and support. Even after you get settled, there may be days when that lonely feeling returns.

During these lonely stretches of time, it is important to take care of yourself. While self-care looks different for each individual, the general purpose is the same: find things that nourish your body, mind, and spirit so you will feel refreshed and strengthened instead of drained. Take a class. Join a gym or yoga studio. Engage in a craft or hobby. Not only can these activities provide fulfillment for you, they are also potential ways to make new friends with similar interests.

The time in between when you've left one friend group and haven't found the next one can be emotionally draining. You may find yourself wishing you were back on a previous assignment where you had a great group of friends and neighbors. You may long for your hometown, or the social life you enjoyed as a student or a young professional. I know I have.

Making new friends is an essential part of feeling settled and happy in your new home. A new place feels strange and lonely until you have a few friends to invite over for a barbecue or to meet up with for a movie or a game. Then it feels like home. Right now, you may not believe this new place will ever feel like home, but eventually it will.

You may be wondering if it's worth the effort to start over when you will move again in a few years. It is worth it, my friend. So worth it. Making friends each time you move pays off a thousand times with rewarding relationships, fun memories, and support when you need it most. At every new location, there will be many others starting over and looking for friends, just like you are. Don't give up.

Sometimes in a new place you will feel lonely for a while, even if you have made a new friend or two. It's natural to miss the connections with friends you have known for years, whether it's your best childhood friend or someone you met at a previous assignment. Loneliness is not always a bad thing. It means you have important people in your life, people who love you and are missing you as much as you miss them. It means you are a loving person and a good friend. You've made many friends in your lifetime, and soon you will build a circle of friends in your new home.

Make the effort to stay connected to friends who are far away. Meaningful friendships will sustain you no matter how much distance separates you. Some of those friendships will last a lifetime, and you may even be stationed with past friends in future assignments.

Making and maintaining friendships in a mobile life can be a challenge. Don't give up; it is worth it! Invest in making connections and friendships, because those connections are one of the best aspects of military life. Your investment in friendship now will pay dividends for many years to come.

Open When
You're Looking for a Job

Dear Job Seeker,

Sending out piles of resumes and sitting through multiple job interviews that end with "Thanks, we'll let you know" can be disappointing and discouraging.

Even if you're new at this, it probably didn't take you long to discover the career facts of military life: your service member's career often takes precedence over your own, and the demands of military life can make it hard for you to find a job or maintain a career.

This is true even if your service member is totally supportive of what you do. Even if you have a degree and experience. And yes, even if you earn more money than your service member.

If it's any comfort, you are not alone in your frustration. Finding a job each time you move can be difficult. Along with having valuable work skills, you'll need to be determined and creative to overcome the employment obstacles military life can put in your way.

Military spouses face difficulties with employment for all kinds of reasons, mostly related to frequent moves: renewing licenses and certifications from state to state, hiring biases against military spouses, childcare issues, and more. Some duty stations simply don't have many job opportunities in the local area. If you are stationed overseas, you may be in a country with laws limiting employment for non-citizens.

Still, it's not impossible for military spouses and significant others to find jobs. First, be aware of the challenges so you can find ways to overcome them. Don't waste energy fighting the circumstances. Instead, think about how to make the most of your current assignment and season of life. If there are few or no jobs at your current duty station, maybe this is a good time to go back to school, get more training, and volunteer for causes you are passionate about. Look for companies open to remote assignments, so you can keep your position as you move. If you are interested in entrepreneurship, you may want to start your own business.

Military spouses have come up with many original and creative ways to work though employment challenges. It may take time, a lot of networking, and a little luck, but there are opportunities out there.

Many organizations and resources are available to help military spouses gain employment. Military spouse hiring preferences for federal jobs can help your resume get noticed. The family center can help you discover all the options open to you. Sign up for online programs to review your resume or give you access to job databases. Seek out a mentor—locally or online—who can help you make connections in your field. Sometimes having a connection makes all the difference.

Can you find employment as a military spouse? Yes, you can, though it might be more challenging than you expect. There are many programs to help and plenty of amazing success stories out there.

I hope you find a great job shortly after your move. But if you can't find work, don't get discouraged. You are still skilled and incredibly valuable. Be innovative and keep trying new things until the right opportunity comes along.

Open When

You Have Questions About Housing

Dear Mobile Military Friend,

In military life, you may not get much say about where you are stationed, but you do have choices when it comes to housing. Will you live in military housing or in the civilian community? You'll find that people have very strong opinions about the pros and cons of military housing, so be sure to ask more than one person. Housing is different at each military base, so experiences may vary.

Trying to find your next home before you move to a new area is certainly one of the bigger headaches in military life. You are probably longing to find the right place and get settled, but you may feel overwhelmed by the military rules about paying for housing. Let's break down and explain the housing budget for military families.

When you are married to a service member, you qualify for military housing if it is available. If you are not married, you cannot live in military housing, no matter how long you have been together, unless you have special permission from their military command.

Active-duty military members qualify for an allowance to help cover the cost of housing. This is called basic allowance for housing (BAH) for those stationed in the United States or overseas housing allowance (OHA) for those overseas. The amount is determined by your service member's rank, the location of their assignment, and family status. Service members with dependents receive more than those without, for example.

When a service member does not live in military housing, their housing allowance is included in their military pay. If you and your service member find a place where the rent is below the housing allowance for that location, you may save a little money each month. If your rent is higher than the allowance, you will have to cover the extra out-of-pocket costs.

If you and your service member live in military housing, your housing allowance will be paid directly to the private housing company that manages military housing, so essentially living in military housing costs the amount of the housing allowance. It is not free, but it is covered completely in the service member's paycheck.

Military housing categories are broken down by rank and number of bedrooms. You will qualify for specific houses based on your service member's rank and the size of your family. Availability of military housing depends on the demand at your location and is not guaranteed. There may be a wait list of weeks or months before a house in your category becomes available. Meanwhile, you will have to find temporary housing elsewhere. Until you move into a military house, your spouse's paycheck will include a housing allowance to help you pay your expenses.

That's the financial angle, but you may wonder what else makes life on a military installation different from life outside the gate? It is different in many ways, and there are pros and cons on both sides. Some families love military housing for the camaraderie and convenience. Others avoid it for the regulations or because they want to invest in their own homes. The right choice for you may depend on your general stage of life: your age, interests, career, children, and so on. There are some locations where living in military housing may be a great fit, and other locations where you may prefer to live in town.

As you might imagine, military housing is populated by military families. This means you will have much in common with your neighbors and many opportunities to make friends. Families with young children will likely find themselves surrounded by other families with kids. When your spouse is deployed, chances are you'll have a neighbor in a similar situation.

Military housing areas are self-contained communities with playgrounds, schools, convenience stores, swimming pools, and gyms all at a convenient—sometimes walking—distance. The cost of housing is also a package deal, including water, trash removal, and average electrical usage. Maintenance crews take care of home repairs, including any appliances provided with the housing.

For some, the downside of life in military housing is being always surrounded by the military. Like everything in military life, housing comes with regulations and requirements about pets, fences, yard maintenance, quiet hours, and what you can leave outside your house or store in your garage. Think of it as a really strict homeowners association.

The age and quality of military housing varies widely from place to place. Some military housing is shiny and new. Other locations may have been built before your mother was born—or your grandmother. These houses may have all the necessities but lack the newest appliances, stylish fixtures, or curb appeal of any kind. In short, with military housing, sometimes you take what is available and make the most of it.

Some people love living on base or post and find the community benefits outweigh the lack of curb appeal. Other people are turned off by horror stories of poor conditions and maintenance or drama with neighbors. In areas with a high cost of living, families may have trouble finding affordable housing and the military option may be the best one. One positive of military housing is that when it's time to move, there's no house to sell and no lease to break.

Some families prefer to rent a home off base because they find it easier to become more involved in the local community. Depending on the location of military housing and where each of you will work, you may find it to be a shorter commute for one or both of you to live off base. If you have school-age children who will attend a public school, you may decide to live in a neighborhood with other students' families to help your children more easily come and go to friends' houses.

Rather than live in military housing or rent a home in a civilian neighborhood, some military families prefer to buy a home and then either sell it or rent it out to tenants when they move to another duty station. This can be a useful long-term investment for some families. Of course, it comes with the responsibility of maintaining a home from a distance.

Every spouse and every family will have different opinions about where to live. A lot depends on the housing costs and quality of military housing at your location, school options for your children, and employment options for you.

If you're feeling overwhelmed with your choices and the need to make decisions quickly, don't panic. Help and information are available. Check social media groups at your new assignment to get the view from those stationed there. Military spouses are adept at sharing information with one another. Real estate websites will help you explore neighborhoods nearby. Compare rental costs and potential mortgage payments. How does it compare to your service member's monthly housing allowance for your location? Don't forget to consider utilities and other expenses, particularly of home ownership, such as maintenance, property taxes, and insurance.

If your children are in school, you will also want to research nearby schools. In addition to opportunities for students, school district offerings can impact housing prices—and resale values if you are buying a home. Consider factors like commute time and reported crime rates in those neighborhoods to make an informed decision.

Deciding where to live is a big decision, and almost any location will have benefits and drawbacks. Military moves give you an opportunity to try out different locations and different kinds of homes to decide which is best for you. When it comes time to leave the military and you're ready to choose your forever home, you'll know more about what you want—and what you don't.

Meanwhile, I hope you find a comfortable place to live, a home you enjoy, and great neighbors!

Open When
You Need a Budget

Dear Money-Cruncher,

Managing money is a struggle for many couples, and military couples are not exempt. Maybe your life has changed a lot recently. When you got married, you probably each had your own income and your own methods of managing money. Now you are learning to combine your income and manage your money together. For many couples, this is not a smooth transition. Financial discussions can feel like a bumpy road filled with potholes and sharp turns. How can you predict what will be waiting around the next bend? And how can you be sure that you and your service member are both steering in the same direction?

Is money management uncharted territory for you? You may have had to leave a job when you moved to join your service member. Or maybe you have a job, but your income is less than your spouse's. You may be uncomfortable if for one reason or another you are contributing less to the family finances than you would like.

Each person in a couple has a right to voice their financial ideas and opinions. Even if you and your spouse don't earn the same amount financially, you should work together to create a budget and agree on spending and saving. You both contribute to your family in different ways. Your family income is for your entire family—even if that's just the two of you right now. Plan for the possibility that it may include others in the future. If you have not created a budget before, there are many financial resources you can use to help you find a spending plan, to balance what you make with what you spend and save.

Having a plan will help you and your spouse get on the same page about your financial goals and how to manage your money. For some couples, it isn't the income that's a struggle but the management of it. Who will pay the bills? How will you spend your money? Usually, one person is more interested in money management than the other. One may be more attuned to saving money and investing for retirement or a college fund. When a big spender marries a penny-pincher, there are bound to be arguments about money. If you are one of these, you probably wish your service member could be more like you sometimes. The good news is that you can use your differences to create balance in your finances. Sometimes you need to spend and sometimes you need to save. The hard work is agreeing on the details of how and when spending and saving should happen.

Creating a household budget is a useful way to discuss finances and get on the same page about money. Budgeting helps you see the money coming into and flowing out of your accounts. It's both a snapshot of where you are right now, as well as a schedule for where you want to be next month, a year from now, ten years from now, or even at retirement. A balanced budget should include both a savings and a spending plan. You need to figure out how much you need to spend, how much you can save, and what you should invest for the future.

Creating a budget can feel intimidating, especially if the military keeps creating change in your life. Moves and deployments can increase spending or income and can cause confusion in your budget.

Moving always involves many out-of-pocket expenses. Even if the military is paying for your movers and your travel, you may still need to buy a vehicle or put down a security deposit for an apartment, expenses the military does not cover. Big ticket items that come with a move can throw off your usual spending plan for months afterwards. Military families, knowing the next move is always coming, are wise to set aside money for the up-front expenses that each move requires.

Deployments also affect budgeting. Sometimes the service member earns more during a deployment, for example if they are in a combat zone receiving hazardous duty pay. Sometimes the service member has little access to the internet and few opportunities to spend money. In other locations, they may have more time and opportunity to travel. They could end up spending more money while deployed than they would if they were home.

Another consideration is who will take care of paying the bills in your family or partnership. In case of deployment, that may change from time to time. If your service member is usually the money manager, you may need to take over that duty during deployment. Be sure you both have full access to your bank accounts and bills.

Understand that a budget is not designed to be set in stone forever. Because your finances may change dramatically with military life events—or if you add children to your family—you and your service member should discuss and re-evaluate your household budget periodically. Any time you are expecting a big change, it's good to have a check-in conversation about the budget.

Like any facet of your relationship, your financial situation needs to be discussed and nurtured regularly. Consider your budget a project where you can both learn and make adjustments. If you are experiencing conflict on this topic, the family center at your military installation may have free budgeting classes or guidance for you.

The way you save and spend as individuals is not just an individual decision. It affects you as a couple and as a family. Running up credit card debt or over-spending from a joint account will reflect on both of you with bad credit and difficult financial situations. Likewise, sound planning and saving will benefit both of you in the long run.

Think of your budget as a puzzle to solve, or a treasure hunt where you are trying to find all the hidden drains on your bank account and ways to keep more money in the bank. Work together to compromise and find a reasonable plan that works for both of you. Planning a budget is something you can do to benefit each other and build your life together. Work together and let your marriage benefit from budget conversations. You and your spouse both have so much to gain when you plan your finances together!

Open When
You're Going to Your
First Military Ball

Dear Diner and Dancer,

Going to your first military ball is so exciting! As with many other events of military life, it can seem a bit mysterious, so let me pull back the curtain on this big event. With a little inside information, you can be prepared, feel confident, and have a wonderful time.

A military ball is a formal event, celebrating your service member's unit and branch. It usually includes a formal ceremony and a sit-down dinner. The ceremony may include the branch song or anthem, a flag ceremony, guest speaker, and tribute to fallen service members. After the ceremony and dinner, there will be dancing, with a band or DJ. Sort of like a very patriotic prom.

As a civilian guest, even if you are a spouse, you are never expected to stand at attention or salute—at a military ball or in any situation. You do need to observe normal civilian courtesies, respect for the flag, and good table manners. During the entrance of the colors or flags and when the National Anthem is played, civilians are expected to stand respectfully. During the National Anthem, you may place your right hand over your heart if you wish. If the anthems and flags of other countries are presented, stand respectfully.

If you're not sure about which fork or plate to use during a formal dinner, or which plate is the bread plate, it can't hurt to read up on that before you go.

What to wear to the ball is always the big question. For a ball, military members will wear their most formal uniform or service dress. As a date, your attire should be equally formal. For women, this generally means a dress, either floor length or knee-length. It doesn't have to be a big puffy ball gown with a train, but it can be if you like.

Think more like bridesmaid dresses you would see at a classy wedding. For men, a tuxedo is fine but usually not required. A suit, including jacket and tie, is considered appropriate.

Sometimes you may attend other military dinners or events that are less formal than a ball. For any event—a holiday party, Dining In, or Khaki Ball, information about appropriate attire will be included in the invitation. When in doubt, ask other dates or spouses what they are planning to wear.

The term "appropriate attire" has a different meaning for everyone. When considering what it means for you at any military event, remember it is a work function for your service member, where you will probably meet their boss or commanding officer, their coworkers and spouses. Ideally, appropriate attire should not expose underwear, cleavage, or midriff. Extremely tight clothing is also revealing—not to mention uncomfortable. Ditto for extremely short skirts. If you have to ask, "Does this show too much?" then the answer is probably, "Yes."

When choosing what to wear, make sure it is comfortable. This includes your shoes. In the course of a long evening, you will do lots of sitting, standing, and dancing. Bring a wrap, particularly if your shoulders are uncovered, because venues—large hotel or restaurant ballrooms—may be chilly in any season.

As for the color of your attire for a military ball, the possibilities are endless, and the choice is yours! You may want to match your date's military uniform or complement it. You may want to wear a unique pattern or bright colors to help you stand out in the crowd.

Be sure to eat a little something before you leave home. Dinner isn't served until the ceremony and keynote speaker are finished, and that can take a while. The bar is usually open at the beginning, and if you want to start the evening with a glass of wine or a cocktail, of course it's better not to have an empty stomach. Even if you don't plan to drink alcohol, you will enjoy the program more if you aren't hungry when you arrive.

The ceremony before dinner is the serious part of the evening. A printed program is usually provided to tell guests when they are expected to stand or sit, as well as describing any special observances, toasts, and songs. During the ceremony, everyone is expected to remain at their tables if at all possible. Visit the restroom and get a drink before the ceremony begins.

You may also have special guests seated at your table, such as decorated veterans, or Gold Star family members who have lost a loved one in military service. These individuals should be accorded an extra measure of respect for their service and sacrifice.

Don't worry if you don't know anyone else at the ball. Your service member will know some people and should introduce you. Be prepared to spend some time alone during the evening if your service member is part of the ceremony or the program. Ask them ahead of time if this is the case.

Then enjoy your dinner and have fun with your military loved one! Go ahead and laugh, make friends, dance, and drink (responsibly). Be sure to take a photo of the two of you! I hope you have a great time at your first military ball!

Open When
You Spend Your First Night Alone

Dear One With All the Pillows,

I can still remember the first night I spent alone after I got married. I came home to a quiet, empty apartment. I ate dinner. I watched TV. It didn't hit me until I went to bed. Stretching out in the empty bed I was used to sharing with my husband, I suddenly felt alone. I also realized the sad truth that I would spend many, many nights like this during my life as a military spouse. That's when my tears started. There I was, a newlywed, with a life full of lonely nights ahead of me.

If fears and feelings like these brought you to this letter, I understand. The uncertainty of military life can be overwhelming for all of us. Here's what I want you to hear: you only ever have to face one night at a time. Many years into my life as a military spouse, I have spent countless nights on my own. I don't cry about them—at least not all of them—because I take each one as it comes instead of worrying about all the ones ahead. Each night is only one night, and I can face one night.

For nights alone, deployments, or any other challenge, don't pile up an entire military lifetime of challenges into a mountain and try to climb it all at once.

Instead, on this night when you are on your own, take advantage of the time you have to yourself. Focus on the silver linings. Do something you enjoy, but your spouse doesn't. What food do you love that your spouse doesn't like? Eat that! What movies or shows do you enjoy that your service member can't stand? Watch that! You may start looking forward to a chance to catch up with your favorite shows.

Give yourself something to look forward to. When you know your spouse will be gone, schedule phone dates with your parents, siblings, or friends. If you have a friend whose service member is also away, invite them over. Make dinner together, watch a fun movie, or just hang out laughing and drinking wine together. You will both enjoy the company and fend off loneliness while building your friendship.

Nights alone are the perfect time to pursue something you enjoy. Create something: write, draw, sew, build, or do home improvements.

If you enjoy cleaning, this is the perfect time to clean house. Some spouses feel the only time their house is clean is when the service member is gone, because then their gear is out of the way and their boots aren't tracking dirt everywhere. If cleaning makes you feel like all is right with the world, then go for it! If not, then take the night off.

Writing can be a therapeutic way to vent your feelings. Write in a journal. Whether it's a prayer journal or a diary, get it out on paper so you don't have to hold the emotions inside. If you don't like to write, consider a video journal to express your feelings.

Know what activities are most likely to help you relax so you can sleep. During the day, take time to exercise, outside if possible. Fresh air can help you sleep better. In the evening, enjoy a hot bath, a favorite book or movie, whatever helps you relax. You won't gain anything with endless scrolling online or lots of tossing and turning in bed. A good night's sleep will prepare you to face a new day.

Yes, nights alone are part of military spouse life, but they don't have to be sad and lonely. There are plenty of great ways to enjoy your time alone. Planning ahead will give you something to look forward to instead of only dreading your loved one's absence.

Maybe the emotions of being on your own caught you off guard on your first night alone. Next time try some of these ideas and make plans. Be intentional about how you spend your time.

And remember, you are never truly alone once you are part of the military community. Plenty of other spouses and significant others are going through this same thing right now. Their support is only a phone call or message away.

Handle With Care

My Story
Big News on a Post-it Note

I paced back and forth in my college dorm room, sobbing and choking back my fears. I looked again at the yellow square of paper, a message from my roommate scribbled on a Post-it Note.

Dan called. He was injured. He'll call back.

Dan, then my fiancé, was halfway through a nine-month combat deployment to Iraq. I had no idea where he was, whether he would recover, or how badly he was injured. My mind flew in a million directions as I imagined the worst. *Would I ever see him again? Had he lost a limb? Would we ever be able to get married?* I was alone with no one to answer my questions. The only information I had was the terrible message my roommate had written down. I paced back and forth with my heart pounding, waiting for the phone to ring.

It was April of my senior year, and this was Dan's second combat deployment within a year. The entire time he had been deployed, I dreaded receiving this kind of news. It was a worry I constantly pushed to the back of my mind, so I could focus on writing papers and finishing classes. I didn't hear from him often, and naturally, I worried constantly about his safety and prayed for him every day.

With the little note in my hand, I paced the room, feeling like I was falling apart. Preparing for finals and writing my senior thesis, I had taken my laptop outside to soak up some sun while I worked. I didn't have a cell phone then, only a landline in my dorm room. Apparently, Dan had called while I was outside. When I returned to my dorm room, the note was on my desk, and my roommate and other apartment mates were gone. I felt completely alone and crushed with the weight of the frightening news and fearful questions.

A short time later, the phone rang again. It was Dan! I was so relieved to hear the sound of his voice.

"I'm okay, but I got blown up," he said bluntly.

After pelting him with questions, I learned he had been standing on a rooftop with his fireteam when an improvised explosive device detonated in a pile of rubble beneath his feet. Shrapnel shot through his boot, tearing a hole through his foot. He was calling from an American military hospital in Germany, where he had been medically evacuated. I wasn't allowed to visit him in Germany, but the military would soon fly him to a hospital in the States where I would be able to go see him.

My tears flowed freely after we spoke, but now they were mixed with feelings of gratitude and relief. He was going to be okay. Knowing that meant I was going to be okay also.

After several surgeries, Dan made a full recovery. First, he used crutches, then a cane. Eventually he was able to walk on his own and then run. The day of his injury was probably the darkest and most terrifying experience either one of us would go through, but we survived. We made it. We both recovered.

Military life is full of twists and turns, some of them very unnerving. At our wedding, the priest told us marriage would often feel like a roller coaster ride, and he was absolutely right. Sometimes military life reminds me of one of those indoor roller coasters where it is so dark you can't see the track ahead. You don't know if you're about to drop down a steep cliff, be spun upside down, or come to a sudden halt. All you can do is hang on and trust in your safety harness. Other times you may emerge into the sunlight, climbing upward with clear blue skies overhead, and the view will be amazing.

The journey of military life has dramatic ups and downs. You may want to scream—out of excitement, fright, or pure frustration. I hope you and your service member are never plunged into the terrifying ride Dan and I experienced with his injury, but there will be other twists and turns.

Other times, military life offers unique, amazing opportunities. In more than two decades with my Marine, military life has held plenty of surprises. The bad news on a Post-it Note was certainly one of the worst, but I've had good surprises too. When we were stationed in Rota, Spain, I wrote a guidebook called *Welcome to Rota*. The local tourism bureau was impressed with it and invited me to present a copy of my book to the mayor in a ceremony at the Rota town hall—a thirteenth century castle. On the morning when I visited the castle and made a presentation in a mixture of English and Spanish, I realized it was an experience I never would have had if I had not said "I do" to military life with Dan.

I do hope military life will hold some pleasant surprises in your future. Who knows what lies ahead around the next turn: An exciting duty station? New friendships and job opportunities? Unique experiences you and your service member will treasure forever? With every twist and turn, military life is full of change and surprises.

There might never be a time when everything is easy. Military life isn't known for carefree coasting. It's more often characterized by steep climbs and sudden drops. Sometimes, however, there are breathtaking views in between. The more you experience, the more you will realize you have what it takes to endure and even enjoy this ride. You have a safety harness—your service member, family, faith, and the network of friends you will make over the years.

This section is all about the unique challenges that come with loving a service member. Whatever the military throws your way, don't be afraid of those moments or your emotions. They are real. You have the strength inside you to ride through both the wonderful and the terrifying moments in military life.

The Military Throws You Curve Balls

Dear Dazed and Confused,

Today you were caught off guard. It might have been good news—a promotion—or bad news—a surprise deployment. The military has many ways of keeping life interesting. Oh sure, you know nothing is ever set in stone in military life. Change is a constant. Your military friends probably joke about never writing in pen on their calendars. You are always prepared with a Plan B, C, and even D. You know your service member serves the needs of the military, and they can be moved, deployed, or given new orders of any kind at any time.

Yes, you know all that. But knowing it and living it are two different things. You weren't expecting this. You didn't think it would happen to you, right now, right here. But here you are, and your mind is spinning.

When something unexpected lands in the middle of your routines, you might feel frustrated, anxious, eager, excited, or apprehensive, depending on the news you received. When the news is bad, even if it isn't really your service member's fault, they are often the first target of your anger, since their job is causing the upheaval. Go ahead and cry. Acknowledge how upsetting it is. Then recognize your service member is on the receiving end of this curve ball too.

You probably think the military has no regard for you and your family. They really don't care how many hoops you have to jump through to deal with this news. It doesn't matter to the military if you are in the middle of a school semester, or pregnant, or ill, or just bought a house, or finally got the kids into a good school. Orders are orders, and whatever they may be, they have to be followed, no matter how inconvenient they are. It doesn't seem fair, and it can be a huge burden for family members to carry.

This news, whether good or bad, may be just as surprising and unsettling to your service member. Like you, they had goals and ideas for the road ahead, and this new situation may not have been part of their plan. They also have to drop everything else to meet the needs of the military. They may be just as frustrated and blindsided by this, with the added burden of guilt because of the effects on you. Whatever the curve ball is, look at it as a challenge you will face together as a team. You may each struggle to adjust to the changes you face, but if you lean on each other, you can get through it together.

Start by asking questions. Even if your loved one doesn't have all the answers yet, get on the same page as soon as possible. Get the available details and make a timeline if you need one. Find out what resources are available to help you adapt and move forward. Tell your service member you support them. Let them know you have concerns, but you are on board.

Be kind to each other and be kind to yourself right now. Handling big change, even good change, creates emotional stress, which can have a huge effect on your body. Don't be surprised if you feel exhausted, overwhelmed, and drained. Get rest when you need it, and don't focus on this one thing all day. Take your mind off this big curve ball and remember the positives in your life.

Possibly your life is about to change a lot, and inside, you may be freaking out. You will make it! One way or another, you and your loved one are going to navigate the changes together, whatever they are. When you feel drained and exhausted, lean on each other. When your service member is struggling to make the right choice, listen to them and let them voice their concerns. By talking through the possibilities and being open with each other, you can face this together.

Yes, this news was unexpected. It may be unsettling or challenging or exciting, or a combination of all those things. You are up to it, and you aren't alone. Lean on your service member and your community. Find inspiration from others and from your own past successes. You have handled so many other challenges. You can do this too! Today, your military life threw you a curve ball. But tomorrow, you will carry on cheering for the team and swinging for the fences.

Open When

You Celebrate Your Birthday Alone

Dear Birthday Star,

Well, happy birthday to you, party of one. You were hoping to celebrate with your loved one, but they can't be with you. Maybe it's not the first time. It's so frustrating when your plans don't work out, and you have every right to feel a little bit disappointed. You certainly would prefer to have your service member with you.

If you love someone in the military, you are bound to celebrate some birthdays alone. But knowing it is a possibility doesn't make it easier to bear when the date comes up on the calendar and your military loved one is away from home. Being alone on what should be a special day is disappointing and frustrating. It's enough to make you want to cry and yell or just stay in bed, because it's no fun celebrating on your own.

Sometimes the loneliness hits a lot harder than usual. Perhaps you already know your service member will be away next year, so you really wanted to have a good time together this year. Or maybe it's a milestone birthday and you really wanted to have a big party. You still can, but it's just not the same without your love.

It's also disappointing if your service member doesn't seem to make any effort to mark your special day occasion. Sure, you know they're busy training or in school or deployed. But you still thought they might call, or send flowers, or at least remember the date with a text. If you don't hear from them on your special day, it can really intensify your feelings of loneliness or disappointment. But not sending a message is not the same as not caring about you. If your loved one is deployed, they may not have good internet access and may not have any way to contact you to celebrate with you.

You won't gain anything from crying about spending your day alone. Face it the best you can and prepare for it with intention.

Sometimes you can't count on other people to make your birthday or anniversary special—not even your loved one. You just have to do it yourself. It might even end up being a fun day, especially if you share it with friends. If you are celebrating a birthday apart, the best thing to do is skip the pity party and throw a real party instead.

This is your day to spoil yourself, treat yourself to something nice, and maybe cross off an item from your bucket list. Grab a friend or two to spend time with you, so you won't feel alone. This year, your best birthday present may have to come from you, and that's great because you know exactly what you want! Eat your favorite foods. Think about what you would enjoy most, book a babysitter if you need one, and then get out there and enjoy yourself for a few hours. You deserve it!

Even if you prefer a quiet evening in, you can still take time to celebrate you. Make a list of all you have done well in the past year. Set new goals, make plans, or simply think about what you are looking forward to in the coming year. Celebrate your accomplishments and your abilities.

This year's celebration is going to be different. You may feel lonely and disappointed because you can't share it with your service member, but this is your chance to create your own celebration and do whatever you want to do. Make the most of this year and hope for the best for next year. I wish you a very fun, creative, and happy birthday!

Open When
You're Angry at the Military

Dear Angry Friend,

It really isn't fair. It isn't fair that the military takes your loved one away for months at a time, that you have to live away from your family, move so often, start over and over again, and make new friends every two or three years. It isn't fair that you to have to give up your career to follow your military spouse, to put your dreams on hold, and put the military first. And it definitely isn't fair that things always break and go wrong when you are on your own!

I know you are tired of all the stress, frustration, uncertain hours, and canceled plans. You may feel at your limit of missed birthdays and anniversaries. Do you feel you are simply fed up with this military life?

At one time or another, every military spouse or significant other feels what you are feeling right now. Not everyone talks about it. Sometimes others put on a brave face and keep marching, but we've all been there. Military life is full of frustrating demands. No matter what anyone tells you, there's no way to know exactly what you were signing up for when you fell in love with a service member. And maybe your spouse wasn't even in the military when you fell in love. Even if you do know a thing or two about military life, there will be days when it just makes you mad.

Your anger is justified. Sometimes this way of life requires so much of you and gives back so little. It stretches you to the limit until you feel you might snap. Has it been a bad day or a tough week? Maybe it's been this whole year. Whatever it is, you're right. It's hard. Go ahead and cry or yell. Vent to a friend or your service member without blaming them. Don't keep your anger trapped inside you. Get it out!

Once you've acknowledged your anger, you have a choice. Stay angry or move forward. Being angry is a natural response to frustrating or unjust situations, but it is rarely helpful until you channel it into positive action. Maybe there is something you can do to make the situation better for yourself or for others. Maybe there isn't. Yes, military life sucks sometimes. If you can't change it, you must learn to work with it. Whatever your situation, sitting in your anger for too long won't help. It's like sitting in a dark room, yelling because you can't see. Your anger won't make the darkness any less severe. But if you feel around for a flashlight or a light switch, you may be able to improve the situation.

Focusing on positive actions or words is a good way to get out of the spiral of anger. Maybe there is something you could do to make the situation better or less frustrating for yourself and others. Many resources and programs that support and advocate for military families were born of anger and frustration channeled into positive action. Channeling those emotions into positive action can feel like switching on a light in that dark room.

You can also look for the humor. Laughter is like a steady beam of light from a flashlight—it brightens everything it touches. Something about this situation is bound to make a funny story someday. Find something to laugh or at least smile about.

Finally, look at the big picture. Moments of anger can be opportunities for growth, if you let them teach you. What can you learn from this experience, so you don't go through it again? Would you handle it differently or have different conversations with your spouse next time?

It's okay to be angry, but don't stay angry for too long. If you stew in your anger, you could hurt yourself or those nearest to you. The healthier choice is to move forward. Search for a light source, and use the energy your anger produces to take action.

Open When
You Love Your Military Life

Dear Contented Friend,

Some of these letters are full of difficult emotions, but that's not how you are feeling today. Yes, today your heart swells with joy and pride, and you sincerely love your military life. That is something to celebrate!

It's definitely okay to be happy and feel good about this life sometimes. You don't have to love every minute of it, and you don't have to like every person on your base, but there are certainly many incredible moments in military life, and you just want to savor them. You love the way your service member looks in their dress uniform. You feel a rush of pride and excitement whenever they put it on. You adore that hug and kiss that comes at homecoming, when the world melts away and your lover's embrace makes all the time apart worthwhile. You appreciate the job security the military provides. When your friends struggle with employment or health insurance concerns, you feel a wave of gratitude that your service member's sacrifices give your family stability. Maybe you enjoy the sense of adventure that comes with military life, the possibility of living overseas and the opportunity to visit new parts of the country. And you probably celebrate the incredible friendships you have made during military life. You will make deep friendships that last as you experience shared events like deployments and PCS moves.

So today, you are basking in the warm glow of contentedness with this lifestyle. And in case you need to hear this, it's okay for you to be happy! You and your service member have both worked hard and made many sacrifices. You have every right to savor the joyous, unique moments that come from the military experience.

Sometimes, people expect military loved ones to feel sad all the time because of the various challenges in this life. Because your service member is away, or you don't live near family, or you change jobs often, you may have family and friends who speak about your participation in military life with a pitying tone. They feel sorry for you, and therefore they expect you to act like you regret your choices. Don't let them get you down.

If you and your service member are happy, then there is no reason to regret choosing military life. It might not be for everyone, but it's working for you. When your service member is away, they want you to continue living your best life, pursuing your dreams, and developing your talents. Your loved one doesn't expect you to sit at home pining away while waiting for the phone to ring! If your service member doesn't have this expectation, then there's no reason society should expect it either.

While there are certainly challenging days here and there, we must admit there are times when military life actually feels easy. You may be coasting along, feeling strong and confident and telling yourself, "I've got this!" When you're riding that emotional high, don't second-guess yourself or question if you're doing things right. Other people might be struggling during that same deployment or PCS move, and it's natural to feel a nagging sense of guilt that perhaps you missed something and should be struggling more. Don't worry, you didn't miss anything. You're just having a good day and someone else is not. We all face our own different struggles at various times. Maybe you are standing on top of a mountain enjoying the beautiful view, while someone else is still struggling to hike up the trail. There isn't a right way or a wrong way to cope with military stress.

If you're handling things well and feeling confident about this life, then hold onto those positive feelings. Celebrate your accomplishments and how far you have come. Allow yourself to feel excited about what the future holds. Sure, you know there will be surprises and unexpected twists or turns on the journey, but that shouldn't stop you from savoring the mountaintop view in this moment. You have every reason to love your military life, so go ahead and enjoy it!

Open When
You Have Trouble Sleeping

Dear Sleepless Friend,

Here you are on another sleepless night, lying awake in the dark, restless, stressed, and wondering about all the uncertainties ahead. If only you could find a way to turn off your brain, quiet all the questions, and get some much-needed rest!

Insomnia seems to be an unfortunate side effect of loving a service member. Your loved one spends many nights away from home, for various reasons, and your bed can feel cold and empty without them. When they are in another time zone, it's easy to get in the habit of waking up every few hours to check your phone for a message. The news headlines can cause all kinds of worry and fear, especially when you don't have a way to communicate.

Sometimes, even when your service member is at home, sleeping beside you, your mind reels in a million directions because of big decisions to make and uncertainties in your future.

Will those orders come soon?

Where will we live?

What happens if the promotion doesn't come through, or if it does?

When is the next deployment coming?

The questions never end, because the military doesn't always offer a lot of answers. One of the unofficial mottos of military life is "Be flexible." It sounds great until your brain starts flexing around thirteen different scenarios, each with multiple contingency plans—in the middle of the night.

It becomes a vicious cycle: lack of sleep will make you more emotional, and the extra emotions will keep you up at night. Something has to change and break the cycle, because you can't keep going like this. Your body can't function for long in this sleep-deprived state.

Unfortunately, there isn't much you can do to change the military.

Worrying won't bring your loved one home a single minute sooner. Waking up every hour won't keep them safe. And no matter how many "what ifs" haunt your mind in the wee hours of the morning, the military is going to keep steaming along, issuing orders for moves, creating wait lists for housing, and deploying personnel.

You can't bend the military to your will. In most cases you can't change the way the military works, but you can change yourself and your responses to military life. You can find your own ways to cope with the stress or loneliness and leave those questions unanswered until tomorrow. You may not be able to force yourself back to sleep, but you can make choices to help you sleep better.

If your service member is away and you keep waking yourself up to check your phone, the first step to better sleep is to work out a healthier communication plan. Time zone differences can be frustrating, but there's usually a way to balance time to talk and time to sleep for both of you. Consider scheduling something on the weekends or at a particular time during the day so you can rest easier at night.

A wind-down routine before bed will help you get ready to sleep. Relax with a peaceful activity such as taking a hot bath, writing in your journal, listening to music or soothing sounds. Breathing exercises can also help you relax. If you're a praying person, a meditation or a repetitive prayer may be helpful.

Disconnect from social media and electronics, including television, before bed. Blue light from screens puts your brain on alert instead of preparing it for sleep. Social media drama might also disturb you when you're trying to relax.

The environment in your room matters too. At bedtime, keep your lights dim, the television off, and your space free from clutter. Aromas such as lavender can contribute to a relaxing bedtime environment. If you have trouble sleeping alone, consider investing in a weighted blanket. It surrounds you with what feels like a warm hug and is effective in calming anxiety.

Alcohol is a common choice for an evening relaxation beverage. However, alcohol contains stimulants that may actually keep you awake longer. If you typically drink a beer or glass of wine in the evenings, consider swapping it for something soothing and more conducive to sleep, such as herbal tea or decaffeinated hot chocolate.

If you have tried all of these methods and still struggle, talk to your doctor before taking any medication to help you sleep. Your doctor will take into account any underlying anxiety or physical conditions. Please never take any prescriptions or medicines that haven't been prescribed for you. Talking to a counselor may help you process worries and emotions and learn healthy practices to fall sleep and stay asleep.

It can be hard to get a good night's sleep when you are living a military life, but you can do it. Your own choices and actions during the day can boost your body's ability to sleep at night. Try adjusting your eating, exercise, and bedtime routines. You don't need to solve everything right now. Sometimes, the only answer to the dilemmas of military life is to be patient and wait. It's hard, but it is worth it. When you teach your mind to save tomorrow's troubles for tomorrow, then you will be able to get more sleep and awaken with the energy to face the next day.

I wish you sweet dreams and deep sleep!

Open When
You Miss Important Family Events

Dear Far-Away Family Member,

Are you going to miss another family event because you are stationed far from family?

There's an ache of living far from home. It's the sorrow of missing another family event, the guilt of not being there when you are needed, and the frustration of the expense of travel. It's a pain that military families experience often.

It's exciting to receive an invitation to a family event such as a graduation, anniversary party, baby shower, or first communion. But when you are stationed far from family, those invitations are bittersweet. Often, you know you won't be able to travel home, so once again you make your apologies, send a gift, throw away the invitation, and wait to see pictures on social media.

It's painful to miss family weddings, funerals, and other important life events. The regret sits heavily on your heart, sometimes even after many years have passed.

Major life events are supposed to be celebrations. Sometimes families are understanding and brush off your apologies when you can't accept an invitation. They know how hard it is for you, but they want you to know you were invited and welcome—and will be missed.

Other times, families are less understanding.

Why aren't you coming? We were looking forward to seeing the kids.

All of your cousins will be there. You will be the only one missing.

Ever since you married into the military, we never see you anymore.

Sound familiar? Major events can be a major pain and a source of family drama. If you are caught in the dilemma of whether or not to go home for family events, take comfort. You may be able to work out a compromise.

If at all possible, and if you want to be there, make the trip. Yes, money is a concern, and sometimes there simply isn't enough in the savings account to buy a plane ticket. Other times, you may be letting the inconvenience and hassle of a major trip get in the way. The trip is almost always worth it. You will only be tired for a few days. Maybe broke for a bit longer. But if you don't go, your regret could last a lot longer. Make the trip. Memories are much better than regret.

If the whole family can't go, send a delegation. If it's an event on your side of the family, go on your own so you don't have to wait on the military to approve leave for your service member. If it is the service member's family, they could attend alone if they want to. Buying one ticket is more affordable than sending the whole family. It would be ideal if you could all go together, but one of you is better than no one going at all.

If traveling with children is the biggest impediment, then ask someone to watch your kids. The military spouse community is amazingly generous. This is especially true in emergency cases, such as a funeral. If you have multiple children, you can reach out to multiple friends to help with childcare for a few days.

If you simply can't attend a family event in person, connect via technology. Don't let the day go by without trying to call or video chat. Let the family pass the phone around for a few minutes, so you can see and speak to everyone and let them know you're thinking of them. Sometimes this is all it takes to feel connected. You really can feel love over great distances, especially when you get to see their faces.

I'm sorry you are struggling with this event, and I wish it were easier to get home any time you wanted. But know that the invitation means your family is thinking of you and loves you. Whether or not you are able to attend, let them know you are missing them too!

Open When

You're Thinking About
Having a Baby

Dear Future Mama or Daddy,

Baby fever is hitting you hard, and you're looking at your service member's training schedule, trying to figure out how and where having a baby will fit into military life. If you are the one who would be getting pregnant, you probably wonder: Is it better to get pregnant before your spouse leaves for a while? How would you manage having a baby during deployment? What if your service member is there for the pregnancy and birth, but misses most of the baby's first year?

If your spouse is the one who would be pregnant, there are even more questions to consider. You both probably wonder how having a baby might impact their military training and career. Would it be better to wait another year or so? Would the next duty station make a difference? Will the schedule get better or worse?

Honestly, there is no perfect time to have a baby during military life. Schedules for moves, deployments, and trainings are often unpredictable and may change at the last moment. Even the best-laid plans can fall apart. Add the frustration of trying to match you or your spouse's fertility cycle to the demands of military training, and it can be very difficult to conceive on any schedule at all. Couples who struggle with infertility often feel doubly challenged by the unpredictable nature of military life. Many find there is no ideal time to conceive, and they simply have to hope for the best.

It's pretty easy to come up with reasons that having a baby doesn't fit into a military life. Having a baby during your service member's deployment is daunting, and it's difficult to care for a newborn on your own. Getting orders to move while either of you is pregnant or taking care of a newborn is a challenging obstacle. Giving birth overseas can be frustrating because you may not have help from family and may need to go to a local hospital in your host nation. If you're pregnant while your spouse is away training, you have to deal with the nausea and fatigue on your own. If the service member misses the baby's first year, they will miss so many milestones. And if the service member gets pregnant, it may mean detachment from their unit, a new job assignment, or a setback in your partner's military career.

Military or not, there is no magical time when you will feel completely ready and prepared to have a baby. Expecting parents almost always wish they had more time, more experience, more money in the savings account. Civilian and military families alike have babies at less-than-optimal times. One way or another, though, they figure it out and make it work. The timing doesn't have to be ideal.

Instead of focusing on all the reasons pregnancy and birth might be difficult, it's more helpful to focus on the big picture and the reasons you want to have a child. Even in less than desirable circumstances, there are plenty of military couples who have children and successfully raise them during one or both parents' time in the military.

If you have a choice, then yes, it's probably better not to give birth during your service member's deployment. It's simpler to have a baby at an assignment when you have more support from family and friends. It's easier to take care of a baby—or kids of any age—when there are two parents in the household. But if you do get pregnant by chance or by choice and the timing is less than optimal, you can overcome those challenges.

Deployment births are common in military families. I know firsthand it isn't easy, but with planning and building a support network, you can get through it and have a beautiful baby.

It's not convenient to move while pregnant (since you shouldn't do heavy lifting) or with a newborn (because they require constant care). Yet, many families have moved mid-pregnancy or with a newborn. It isn't easy, but you have the strength and the ability to get through it, one task at a time.

Having a baby overseas is not simple. I've done that too. Even if your family can't come, you won't be alone. The overseas military community tends to be tight-knit, and your friends will come alongside and be your family. It won't be the same as having your own family nearby, but military families often have children while living far away from their families. Large military installations have hospitals with the same quality of care you would receive in the States. If you have to deliver at a local hospital in another country, military healthcare will cover either an English-speaking doctor or a translator to help with the delivery. Even though it may be daunting, you are in good company. Procedures are in place to take care of you and your baby if you give birth while stationed overseas.

You may wonder how your baby will bond if your service member is deployed or away for repeated temporary duty (TDY) assignments. Babies and young children will likely cling to you and take some time to get used to their service member parent if that parent is away for extended periods. However, most babies adjust quickly. The more they can see pictures or video and hear the service member's voice, the easier it will be for babies to adjust. Video chats and video recordings of the absent parent are both helpful to acquaint the baby with the sight and sound of your service member. If your service member is constantly coming and going because of training, it will be harder on you than it will be on the baby. Since babies don't have a sense of time, they don't realize their missing parent is sometimes there and sometimes gone. Yes, the service member will miss some precious milestones and first moments, but thankfully many of these can be captured and sent as pictures or videos.

If your service member gets pregnant, they may experience changes in their job. Active-duty pregnant service members will not be scheduled to deploy and may be put on light duty or assigned a different military occupational specialty (MOS) during pregnancy if their current job is hazardous. They may wear a different uniform to accommodate body changes during pregnancy and have reduced PT requirements for a year after the birth. Maternity leave requirements vary by military branch, but each one supports paid maternity leave, and every branch is required to make accommodations for a service member who chooses to nurse their baby. It may not be easy, and there are times your partner may need to reach out to a superior, but your service member will likely find support from fellow service members who have already been though this experience.

Military life can make family planning more difficult, but every challenge can be managed or overcome. You may not be able to plan the perfect time to have a baby, but you can find the best options for your family. Ultimately, you and every new parent can plan all you want, but you can only cross each bridge as you come to it. Don't worry too much about your schedule, because after the baby is born, it will change forever anyway.

There's no perfect time to have a baby, but the right time is when you and your spouse decide you want to add children to your family, or when nature decides for you. You will figure out how to make it work. Ask other parents for advice and resources, lean on your community for support, and don't be afraid of the challenges. Being a parent is a new adventure all its own. Deciding when to have a baby is just the start. Just like every new parent, even if you aren't sure what to do at first, you have all the strength and skills to figure it out. When you have a new baby in your arms, no matter what you've been through to get there, it will all be worth it!

Open When
You Want to Go Back to School

Dear Potential Student,

You're considering starting a new certification or degree program, and you're wondering how you will fit it into your military life. I applaud you for working on your education and improving your skills! As well as opening up new employment possibilities for you, it will give you opportunities to pursue something you love while using your gifts and talents—all this plus possibly putting more money in the bank. Going back to school is a big step, one you should definitely be proud of!

As you're considering this path, you're probably seeing a few challenges. Perhaps you are trying to figure out how to fit classes and homework into your current job schedule and also take care of your kids. Maybe you wonder how you will pay for tuition. Or perhaps you just aren't sure how your programs will work if your service member is deployed or gets orders to move.

You might choose to attend a nearby college, university, or training program. Some universities offer degree programs through extensions at military installations. Online options open up many courses of study and are less affected by a change in location or schedule. Online classes also offer more schedule flexibility, so you can adapt your classes to your work, the needs of your kids, and your service member's absences.

Working on a flexible schedule requires discipline on your part. Even though you can do your schoolwork almost any time and anywhere, you still have to make time and space to do it. What will you have to give up to allow yourself the hours you need for school each week? Make sure you and your service member are organized and clear on your priorities before you commit to classes and tuition.

Another consideration is how you will pay for school. Review your budget with your spouse and be realistic about how many classes you can take and what payment timeline will work for you. Part of the financial consideration may be the need for a regular sitter or other household help while you work toward your goal.

To help pay for your classes, you can find scholarships and tuition assistance programs especially for military spouses at the local and national levels. Eligibility requirements vary. Visit your installation education center for information about financial assistance. Look outside the military community too, for scholarships based on academic merit, your field of study, life experiences, ethnicity, and more. Fill out a Free Application for Federal Student Aid (FAFSA) to see if you qualify for federal grants or loans.

Maybe it has been a while since you were in school, and you are wondering whether you can make the grade. Perhaps you struggled in school before. Or maybe someone in your life has discouraged you from getting your degree. It's time to stop listening to those voices. Set goals for yourself and don't look back. If you suspect a learning issue has held you back in the past, don't hesitate to seek a diagnosis, treatment, and techniques to overcome it.

Even though you really want to go back to school, you may be second-guessing the timing of your decision, wondering if you should wait until after the next move, or when a deployment is over. But there may never be a perfect time to take on a new class schedule or heavy homework load, and all that goes with it. There will always be other commitments and circumstances of military life that will discourage you if you let them. If you want to go to school, don't put it on hold waiting for a time without a deployment or a move. All you can do is work around life as it happens. During a deployment could actually be an excellent time to go back to school. Your classwork will give you focus, definite goals, and will more than fill the time you would usually spend with your service member.

Military life is unpredictable, but you don't have to defer your dreams. Your goals matter, and you can fulfill them. If going back to school is important to you, find a way to make it work. One class at a time, one project at a time, you will inch closer to your goal. Keep moving forward, because you have a lot to be proud of! When you have sacrificed for your education, you will feel the satisfaction of having truly earned it. Then you will see your hard work pay off with open doors and exciting opportunities. So buckle down and get ready for this big adventure. You've got what it takes, and you can earn this!

Open When
You've Been Insulted

Dear Hurting Friend,

Sometimes people just don't think before they talk. Sounds like you experienced that today, when someone decided to comment on military life and insult you or your service member.

Maybe they meant well by asking about how deployment was going or when you are going to move again. But all it did was upset you and make you feel helpless in this difficult lifestyle.

Maybe they thought they were giving you good advice or setting you straight.

You knew what you signed up for.

You're not special, lots of people have difficult jobs.

That's military life. Suck it up, Buttercup.

None of these are helpful at all, but we hear them all too often, sometimes from close friends and family members.

Maybe the person who insulted you didn't mean well at all. Maybe they were just plain mean, inconsiderate, or thoughtless.

Someone may have singled you out for a political debate because you love someone in the military. They may assume you must automatically support the president and everything the military has ever done throughout history.

Ugh. These comments are hurtful and exhausting, and I wish I could tell you eventually you'll stop hearing them. Unfortunately, as long as you are connected to a service member, someone, somewhere is going to have an opinion about it. And they will sometimes feel compelled to share those opinions with you.

No, it isn't right. It's rude. But it happens. The best thing to do is to prepare yourself now and be ready to respond next time.

You might feel brave enough to toss a sarcastic comment right back to an outspoken stranger, informing them they don't know anything about your family's situation or sacrifices. But no matter how clever your comeback, sarcasm really isn't the best response. It will likely make you feel angry and bitter for the rest of the day. And it certainly won't open the stranger's eyes to the truths of military life.

It's more satisfying to take the high road. Respond by saying, "I'm proud of my service member and all their sacrifices," and walk away. If the person is perceptive, they will realize their comments are hurtful and may think twice before making them to you or to anyone. On the other hand, you don't have to respond at all. It's not your job to explain military life to people who don't want to listen.

When the insulting comments are coming from a friend or family member, sarcasm is an even worse idea. It will drive a wedge into your relationship, making it difficult for either one of you to respect or encourage the other person. If you want to maintain this relationship, you have to find a way to talk through differences and help them see their comments are hurtful.

Be honest. Explain why their comments aren't helpful and why it's painful for you to hear them. Sometimes people don't realize how their words affect others. You may have to stand up and let them know rather than put up with hearing it repeatedly. If you think they meant well, then tell them what would be supportive instead of hurtful.

Exercise compassion. Military families don't have a corner on all the suffering in the world. In fact, many other people experience loneliness, grief, financial struggles, long-distance relationships, and more. Is it exactly the same as your situation? Probably not, but their situation may not be easier than yours. Everyone carries their own struggles in this life, and they are often invisible. If someone compares your deployment to their spouse's business trip or says you shouldn't be upset because at least your loved one is still alive, try to respond compassionately. You can be suffering, and they can be suffering too. Comparing painful situations doesn't make anyone hurt any less.

Everyone has their own burden of pain and suffering. You can't tell by looking whose burden is heavier or how long they will have to carry it. The weight of your pain has absolutely no effect on the weight of anyone else's, and you don't diminish your own struggles by acknowledging someone else has their own.

If the same person makes a habit of making hurtful comments to you, don't engage in a debate or conversation. It's better to avoid toxic conversations and find support from people who understand. Surrounding yourself with a supportive military community is essential for getting through these uncomfortable moments. Your friends will allow you to vent and will understand what you are going through. You will feel more relaxed around others who have heard similar comments and lived through them.

It is okay to cut ties with toxic family members or friends. If someone truly doesn't respect you and your relationship, then you may not need them in your life right now. It doesn't have to be permanent. It may be the healthy decision to block someone on social media or not take their phone calls for a while. Clearing away their negative comments will help you save your strength for more important conversations and uplifting relationships.

Dealing with stupid comments and insults is unfortunately part of military life. You can't control what people say to you, but you can control yourself. You can choose how to respond. Instead of saying something angry in reply, think about ways to prevent the situation from happening again. Sometimes using words is effective, sometimes not. There are situations where you can just use your feet to walk away.

I'm sorry you had to hear those comments today. But you are awesome, and you did not deserve them. Keep on loving your service member and ignore those who don't understand!

Open When
You Don't Feel Welcome

Dear Snubbed One,

You felt left out and excluded. Maybe you had no one to talk to at a gathering, while everyone else seemed to know each other. Maybe you weren't invited at all. Even worse, someone may have singled you out to ridicule or belittle you. Sometimes, the military community can be the most welcoming and helpful group of people, unified by tight bonds of brotherhood and sisterhood. Other times? Not so much. Whatever happened, I'm sorry you were hurt. You may feel lonely right now, but you are not alone.

There are many reasons you may feel like an outsider. Perhaps you are a girlfriend or boyfriend and not invited to spouse events. Even if you are married to your service member, you may feel excluded because of your spouse's rank or career field. You may feel set apart because of politics, religion, or the size of your family. Sometimes it happens because of cliquish behavior among other spouses. In any group, military or civilian, there will always be some who try to elevate themselves by excluding others, and some who thrive on drama. And sometimes those groups overlap. These people may be military spouses or they may be civilian families in your community, even at church.

No matter who they are, don't let them affect your confidence in yourself. You are who you are, a person with many shining qualities. No petty group of people can change you. If you are feeling rejected or lonely or if a group isn't including you, you haven't found the right group. You can give them a second chance if you like. Anyone can have a bad day, but if you try again and still feel unwelcome or excluded, you don't have to keep coming back. Look for another group instead.

The great thing about military communities is the diversity of people and ways to get involved. There are groups for almost any activity: military girlfriends, military fiancés, book clubs, running clubs, parent groups, Bible studies, volunteer groups, hiking clubs, and wine clubs. Find one where you are comfortable. Don't try to settle into a group that doesn't make space for you. If you think you're in the right group, but aren't being treated the way you deserve, then speak up. Sometimes people don't realize they are making others uncomfortable or leaving people out. If they are still not welcoming, then cut your losses and try another group. You don't need negativity in your life.

If you are a girlfriend, boyfriend, or engaged to a service member, you are connected to military life, although in a different way than a spouse. For practical reasons, membership in installation spouse clubs is generally not extended to those who are dating or engaged to someone in the military. But there are organizations and groups especially for significant others who are not married to their service members. Anyone who loves someone in the military shares much in common with others, whether spouses or significant others. You all have the same joys and challenges of military life; you are simply at different stages of this life, with different needs and interests.

The best way to find support is to find a group where you have common ground. If you are not able to join a spouse group on the base or post, join a support group online where you can make connections with other military loved ones. You might be able to find a group in your area where you can make in-person connections.

No matter who you are, even if you are feeling left out and lonely, you are not alone. Everyone, even the general's wife, feels left out sometimes. It may just be part of being new at your location, but maybe you're not the only new one. Look around and find someone else who is new. Introduce yourself. Get to know them. In military life, every friend is a treasured resource. When you're not the new one, be the one to welcome someone who is new or looks like they need someone to talk to.

Whatever happened to you, I hope you won't let a bad experience stop you from seeking out and making good friends in military life. For every bad apple, there are plenty more sweet and generous ones who are willing to share their time, talents, and resources. Keep looking and you will discover amazing people in the military community.

Open When
You Feel Disconnected
From Military Life

Dear Distant Military Friend,

Support is hard to find when you feel cut off and disconnected from military life. Perhaps you don't live near a military installation, and your civilian neighbors or friends have no clue what you are going through. Or maybe you do live in or near a military community, but you're having trouble getting plugged in and haven't found a place where you feel comfortable.

It's incredibly lonely to face each day on your own, alone in a crowd, when no one around you sees or shares your struggles. You may be feeling this way if your loved one is in the National Guard or a reserve component and you live hours from the nearest base or post. Or you may find yourself in this situation if you moved to be near family or friends during deployment. Even in a loving and supportive environment there may be times you need to talk to someone who shares your military experiences.

Being disconnected—either by geography or circumstances— is challenging. You may feel like an outsider in your civilian world or military world. You probably feel out of place with your civilian neighbors, who may have known each other for years. Also you are dealing with unique military struggles they may not understand. At the same time, you may feel forgotten or overlooked by the military community, where you would like to find a spouse group to rely on for support and information.

Each community—civilian and military—may assume you are being supported by the other. Until you tell them, they probably don't know you need or want connection with them. I know you get tired of having to take the first step, but if no one knows you feel disconnected, then you have to be the one to speak up. Connecting and creating your support system is up to you. It's an effort, but when you find those connections, you won't be on your own anymore. Contact your service member's family leader, usually called an FRG leader or ombudsman. They can update you on events for spouses and kids.

No one should face the challenges of military life alone! Thousands of military families such as yours, and equal numbers of civilian families, would love to help you. You can find online communities of spouses, which might also lead you to a local connection. Even if you don't connect in person, communicating through social media will offer you a measure of support.

When looking for supportive groups online, scroll through the recent discussions on the page to see what type of questions are typically asked and how helpful people are in their responses. If it seems too catty or drama-ridden, move on to another group. There are plenty of online communities filled with kind military spouses who sincerely want to help each other and answer your questions.

To invest in your local community, stop considering yourself an outsider and step in. Being connected to the military doesn't make you any less of a citizen in your town or neighborhood, even if you are only there for a couple of years. Find your people by joining a local gym, church, wine-tasting club, or book group. Become a volunteer at a food bank or for the Red Cross. It will take time, but you will find connections. Your local friends may not know anything about the military at first, but when they get to know you, they will be there to help and support you as a caring friend and a listening ear.

If you don't live near a military installation, you still have access to military resources and support. You can shop military exchanges online, and you don't have to drive to a base or post to find programs offering deployment support. Many national organizations such as the Armed Services YMCA, the USO, and United Through Reading support families across the country, no matter where they are located. Many more programs and companies offer military discounts. Support is available, even if you don't live in a military community. You can also make connections by volunteering for one of these organizations.

Many faith groups and nonprofits are also willing to support military families. If you reach out and share your story, you will likely find a kind team of volunteers who will be there for you on the hard days. In emergencies, it really doesn't matter whether or not someone else has experienced military life. What matters most is their friendship, generosity, and willingness to help your family. As you build up your support system, cast a wide net. You will be surprised how many kind souls are out there!

In military life, there are times when we feel like we don't belong anywhere. The truth is, we can belong everywhere. We may just have to try a little harder to find the best way to fit in. You have the opportunity to create lasting relationships in your military and civilian communities. Don't be afraid. Reach out and keep looking until you find your people. You can build your own village anywhere.

Open When

You're Envious of Other Couples

Dear Green-Eyed Friend,

It happened. You saw a random couple in public, walking along, holding hands, just being happy together, and then *Bam!* out of nowhere, you suddenly felt more resentment and jealousy than you ever thought was possible to feel toward total strangers.

The rational part of your brain knows you should be happy for them. After all, they haven't done anything to you. But the emotional side of your brain is screaming.

How dare they be happy when my lover is so far away?

They look so carefree when I am so stressed. It's not fair!

And even though you know it doesn't help, you have already started crying, and it is really hard to stop.

You don't need to feel guilty for having these confusing emotions. It may be an extension of your pain from being separated from your loved one. It can be overwhelming at times, so much that it causes you physical pain. During deployments and long training cycles, the empty ache in your gut never seems to go away. It may also be because you suspect this couple doesn't have to deal with the frustrations of military life, an upcoming move, and leaving behind family and friends.

It's okay. You're allowed to feel sadness, loneliness, envy, even anger. The emotions are not a problem; it's what you do with them that matters. Emotions are healthy and necessary, as long as they don't control your actions. You can decide how to handle strong feelings. When ugly emotions come—and they will—be prepared and know what to expect. In a peaceful moment, store up some ideas and strategies to use when envy and anger rear their ugly heads.

When you first experience a wave of envy or aching anger against another couple, allow yourself a moment to feel the emotion. Take one moment, but that's all. The emotion itself is natural and shouldn't be ignored or suppressed. Denying your anger when you really are quite upset will only make it worse. Is it hard to attend a wedding or celebrate a holiday without your loved one? Certainly! Is it frustrating to be separated because they are away at training? Of course! Give yourself a moment to admit exactly how you are feeling: envious, angry, lonely, unloved, ugly, whatever. Feel it, but don't dwell on it.

Take a breath and acknowledge what is causing your feelings. Why did a sweet, unassuming couple you don't even know cause such a negative reaction? Do they bring up a memory? Are you especially sad because it's been a really long time since you got to hold your loved one's hand? Be honest with yourself, even in the middle of an ugly emotion. It's okay to admit you feel lonely at a wedding because you wish your service member could be there with you. Putting your reaction into some context will help you to examine your feelings and find where they come from. It will also help you move forward and not get stuck in your anger. The happiness of another couple doesn't in any way diminish what you and your significant other have.

Focus on the positives in your relationship with your loved one. You share a strong love that has been tested over time and distance and has grown stronger as a result. Your love may not always get to express itself with flowers and kisses. That's why you know the amazing joy of hearing their voice for the first time in weeks and the value of old-fashioned handwritten letters. Together you've had new experiences, been to new places.

You have a stockpile of wonderful memories, plenty of good times to savor and more to look forward to. You have a military member who fights to protect this country, and you are darn proud of that! Plus they look really great in their uniform.

Once you focus on your positive memories, you should be feeling a little calmer and more in control. This is a good time to repeat a phrase or mantra to help you focus on the positive and let the negative emotions pass. Choose meaningful and positive words to bring to mind when something triggers negative emotions.

You could say, "I'm happy for them." Even if you don't quite mean it sincerely the first time, keep repeating it until you believe it is true.

You can appreciate the joy of any happy couple. Wait for your heart to agree with your mind, and then move on happily through your day.

You can also say, "Soon, that will be us." When someone else's public displays of affection break your heart, remember your time will come! Deployment and training operations are only temporary. You have the rest of your life to enjoy hand-in-hand walks with your significant other.

True love is not jealous. It helps me to remember I Corinthians 13:4, a Bible passage describing the qualities of love:

Love is patient, love is kind. It does not envy, it does not boast, it is not proud. (NIV)

The rest of the chapter also says true love rejoices in truth and can endure anything. In your true love for your significant other, there is also room for you to rejoice with other couples and wish them the best in their relationships. You can endure hard times together.

When you can, talk about your feelings with your spouse. They are your biggest support and best reminder of the love you share. No struggle of military life lasts forever, even if it seems like it.

If the waves of envy are hitting you worse when you're on social media, then it may be time to cut back on your scrolling. Don't compare your life or your relationship with what you see there anyway. They are images carefully chosen to represent mostly the best. Everyone is facing their own battles, just as you are, but those images may not make the highlight reel on social media.

Online or in person, envy is a difficult thing to handle throughout military life. Some days, you will feel you have more to bear than other people, and sometimes you might be right. But everyone you meet is facing their own battles, even if you can't see them from the outside.

This battle is yours, and you will find a way through it. In the end, other people's happiness can only take away yours if you let it. If you choose instead to accept your emotions, not dwell on them, and then find what you have to be thankful for, you will prevail. Let those images inspire you toward your own happiness!

Open When
You Feel Out of Control

Dear Spinning Friend,

So much about military life is beyond your control, and it's hard. Are you waiting on orders to move, frustrated by not knowing where you will live or work next year? Are you sad because you live so far from your family, or your kids aren't adjusting well to the new place? You may be exhausted because your loved one is deployed, and you can't stop thinking about them or worrying about them.

On a good day you are able to go about your business and function just fine, but that knot of worry is always there in the background, tugging at the dark corners of your mind, challenging you with impossible questions and worst-case scenarios. It keeps you awake at night. It prevents you from having fun, even when you're surrounded by friends. Anxiety can threaten to overwhelm you at various times throughout military life. Navigating this lifestyle sometimes feels like trying to build a tower on shifting sand. One moment you are making progress and feeling hopeful. Then the waves come in, wash away what you have created, and you don't even know where to begin again.

Of course, it's normal to worry about what you can't change or control. But just because worry is normal doesn't mean it's good for you. And on those bad days when there are horrible stories in the news and it hits too close to home, stress can make it difficult to breathe.

Whatever is beyond your control, I'm sure you know worrying won't change it. No matter how much you lie awake at night or walk the floor, your anxiety won't change how long your loved one is deployed or what difficulties they will face. You can't keep your kids—or yourself—from missing friends and family who are far away. You can't make those orders for your next move show up any sooner. Some situations are completely out of your hands.

Keeping your eyes and your mind on those circumstances will not help. The best thing you can do for yourself is to let go of what you can't control and focus on what you can control.

You can control your breathing. Deep breathing and other relaxation techniques are a good way to step off the stress escalator. Listen to soothing music. Get away from social media for a while.

You can't control what's on the news, but you can turn off the television. If your latest bout of stress is coming from a recent news cycle, then turn off the TV and stop scrolling through your social media news feed. What's on the news probably isn't your reality right now, and even if it is, your anxiety will not change it or help you.

Reach out to someone you can talk to, whether near or far. Who is the best listener in your life? Your mom, dad, sibling, a military spouse friend? Connect with them for a chat, either on the phone or in person. Another supportive person can help ground you and take your mind off your fears.

Daily routines are also comforting, especially if you include soothing and calming practices such as writing in a journal, reading an inspirational book, praying, or taking a walk each day. Keeping a daily routine offers a measure of predictability each day.

Small projects will give you something solid to wrap your arms around and also give you a sense of accomplishment. Reorganize a closet, finish a craft project you've started, plan your weekly menu, or create a new fitness routine. Start with something small and build up to more ambitious undertakings.

When you find even one small thing you can control, you may find the other parts of life will start to calm down a bit, too. Start small, gaining confidence with one tiny habit at a time. Then when you are able, add another small habit or routine. You can't control the events of military life, but you can keep your worries from controlling you.

Open When
Your Service Member Is Injured

Dear Worried Friend,

Most service members go through their entire military career without a severe injury, but we know it can happen. If your loved one is not injured but you are worried about the possibility, you are not alone in your fears. If your loved one has been injured, or if you are anxious and would like to prepare for the possibility, this letter is for you.

You may have received the difficult news of your loved one's injury from a chilling phone call after a period of radio silence during deployment, or out of the blue when you just saw your service member a few hours ago. If you are living through this right now, I wish I could envelope you in a giant hug and help you feel strength and peace in this confusing whirlwind. The biggest consolation in the midst of any bad news in military life is that you do not have to go through it alone.

In most cases, military loved ones learn about an injury by phone. The news may come from the service member directly, if they are able to make a phone call, or it could be from an officer in their command. Injuries are scary and confusing. You will have a lot of questions, and there may not be answers right away. Take some deep breaths and know the military is going to take care of your service member with some of the best medical resources on the planet.

If your service member is wounded overseas during a deployment, they will receive emergency treatment right away and then be transferred quickly by a medical evacuation team to the nearest military hospital for treatment. American military hospitals in locations around the world stand ready at all times with specialized care for all kinds of injuries and traumas. Your injured service member will be treated by a team of experts and surgeons trained to handle military injuries. If your loved one will remain in a medical facility—even overseas—for more than a few days, spouses and other family members may be allowed to visit. You can discuss this with the military chain of command to work out details about getting flights and lodging.

In most cases, when a service member's injuries have been stabilized, they will be transferred to a military hospital in the United States. Your loved one will be transferred to the location where they will receive the best care for their injury, not necessarily to the hospital nearest you. As a result, they may not be near where you live or near their duty station. You and other family members will be able to visit, depending on your loved one's condition. If your loved one will be hospitalized for an extended time, you may be able to stay at a Fisher House. Located near most major military hospitals, Fisher Houses provide free lodging for the families of injured military members.

Your service member will be treated by a team of medical experts throughout their journey to recovery. This may include surgeons, doctors, nurses, physical therapists, and more. At every step, they will discuss treatments and options and help you make informed decisions together. Of course, going through an injury can be life-changing, and it's normal to have waves of emotions in response. Depending on their treatment plan, there may be a lot of medication, many details to track, and numerous decisions to make. Of course, you are relieved and grateful when they are with you again, but sometimes you will feel completely overwhelmed, especially when you have the important duty of being your loved one's advocate. You may be the one who coordinates the care they receive from multiple healthcare professionals.

It can be a heavy burden to have all this on your shoulders. You are strong, but you don't have to carry it all by yourself. Lean on the medical teams and on your community for support. They want to help you through this.

Your friends and family may not know how to react to the news of an injury. Some may blurt out the wrong words or ask inappropriate questions. Other people may clam up, so fearful of saying the wrong thing that they say nothing at all. You may feel some people are walking on eggshells when they approach the topic with you.

Whether or not your service member has visible injuries, they may have invisible injuries such as traumatic brain injury and posttraumatic stress. These injuries don't always come with a notification, a medical evacuation, or a date on the calendar, but they still require diagnosis, treatment, and time for healing.

No one knows how to handle an injury of any kind until it happens to them. Forgive those around you when they do or say the wrong thing. Most likely they mean well and want to help. Tell them clearly what would lighten your load. Maybe you could use practical help such as babysitting or meals, or maybe you simply need someone to listen and let you cry. People really do want to support you as you go through this. Reach out and let them know how they can help, even if it feels awkward at first. If you are usually the strong one who helps other people, it may be hard to admit you are the one in need of support. Do the hard thing: let people know what you need. It's good and healthy to ask for help when you need it and accept it when it is offered.

Take comfort in knowing you are part of an incredibly supportive and loving community. As well as individuals, your friends and family, numerous organizations and resources are available to support you and your service member on the road to recovery. The process of adjusting to a new normal after an injury can be a long journey, but you don't have to do it all at once. You only have to face one day at a time and one decision at a time.

Wounds and injuries of any kind are among the most difficult challenges a military loved one can face. If you are facing that news now, then I send you all my love because I know firsthand how terrifying it can be. I also know you can move forward through this, one step at a time. You will not have to handle this alone. Reach out to your community and ask for support, and you will be comforted and uplifted by their response.

Open When
You Want to Pray

Dear Faithful Friend,

There's nothing like the constant change of military life to make you realize you can't handle everything on your own. Maybe it has been a while since you talked to God. Or maybe you are so angry with God and this whole situation that you don't know where to begin.

Military life can be the perfect time to grow in faith or to start praying if you've never prayed before. This life will challenge you to trust in a greater power when everything is up in the air. There will be quiet moments where you feel alone and miss your service member and wish you had someone to talk to. That can be a perfect time to pray, because prayer is simply talking to God, who loves you more than you can imagine.

You may feel overwhelmed and overworked. Adding prayer to your daily to-do list may feel like one more task you simply don't have time for. But the times when you are stressed and weighed down with the demands of life are usually the times prayer can be the most uplifting. It can be very simple. You can associate prayer with a habit you do every day, such as drinking coffee, brushing your hair, or doing dishes, and be mindful of God's presence while you're doing it.

There is power in prayer. God is there all the time, waiting to give you strength for what you need to face. No matter how busy you are, no matter how long it has been since you said a prayer or attended a worship service, God is always there, ready to listen. You only need to slow down long enough to talk to him and accept His love.

There's no right or wrong way to pray. It's simply a conversation, and you can do it anytime. Choose a few quiet moments either in the morning or at night. Ask God to bless your day, be with your loved ones, or to lift the worry from your mind.

Find a devotional book you like and read from it each day. There are many devotion books written especially for military life that speak directly to the struggles you face.

Writing a prayer works as well as speaking it. Keep a journal or a notebook to write down daily thoughts, worries, or decisions you want to tell God about. You can also include gratitude in your writing. Each day, list three things you are thankful for, then thank God for them.

There are many devotional books for couples that you and your service member can read through together. Even during times of limited communication, you can discuss it in letters or messages.

Read a selection from the scripture each day. You may be surprised to discover how God's word speaks to your situations and concerns.

Choose a few encouraging passages. Write them on notecards and post them where you will see them every day and hear God's encouraging words for you. Here are some that have been meaningful to me in my Christian faith.

Trust in the Lord with all your heart and lean not on your own understanding; in all your ways submit to him, and he will make your paths straight. Proverbs 3:5-6 (NIV)

I can do all this through him who gives me strength. Philippians 4:13 (NIV)

Have I not commanded you? Be strong and courageous. Do not be afraid; do not be discouraged, for the Lord your God will be with you wherever you go. Joshua 1:9 (NIV)

God is our refuge and strength, an ever-present help in trouble. Therefore, we will not fear, though the earth give way and the mountains fall into the heart of the sea, though its waters roar and foam and the mountains quake with their surging. Psalm 46:1-3 (NIV)

Praying may feel awkward to you at first, especially if it is a new habit for you, but stick with it. Even if you start with two sentences, or five minutes, adding prayer to your life will make a difference. Sometimes turning to God is the only way to face the challenges of military life. When you find a prayer style that works for you, it will become a calming ritual to help you get through each day.

Military life is hard, but you don't have to do it alone. God is there with you every step of the way. Listen to him, and he will give you his peace and strength. God bless you on your prayer journey!

Open When
Your Marriage Needs
Extra Encouragement

Dear Wife or Husband,

A military marriage is not easy. Even when you absolutely love each other. Even when you are both completely faithful. Even when you are each trying every day to do your best and help your partner. Military life will challenge and stress your marriage in numerous ways, and it's natural for one or both parties to struggle during certain seasons.

Perhaps this is a season of struggle for you. Maybe you and your service member are going through big changes—preparing for a PCS move or an upcoming deployment. You may have recently lost a job, decided to go back to school, or learned that you are expecting a baby. These major events, even if they are anticipated or joyful, certainly add extra stress and uncertainty to a marriage. The military seems to challenge every married couple to stay on their toes with major life changes every few years, constant adjustments, time apart, and layers of communication challenges. The roller coaster of military life means you are constantly either preparing for a big change or recovering from a recent one. The result can leave you feeling rather dizzy, hoping for a steady moment to just catch your breath.

On the other hand, perhaps there are no major looming events this year, but you can't help feeling that your marriage has been struggling lately. There isn't one large problem you can point to. Instead, it just feels like a multitude of minor issues, unkind words, and misunderstandings that have piled up into an uncomfortable iceberg floating near the center of your marriage. There seem to be invisible walls between the two of you, and you aren't sure where they came from or how to climb over them. The problems don't seem serious enough to require professional counseling or a serious sit-down conversation, but you do miss the easy close friendship that you and your spouse always shared. You wonder if this is the natural progression of growing older. Have you fallen out of love? Will you become a boring old married couple with a lukewarm marriage?

Friend, while I can't give you the answers to your own personal relationship challenges, I can assure you of this—every marriage goes through stressful seasons. It doesn't matter if it is a military couple or if neither has anything to do with military service. It doesn't matter how many children you have, what jobs you have, where you live, or how often your service member is gone. Every couple experiences certain levels of stress and challenges because, well, being an adult is full of stressful difficulties. There will always be bills to pay, decisions to make, and differences in opinions. Spending your adult life with another person means that you are bound to encounter some of these difficulties along the way. Disagreements are not necessarily a sign of a failing marriage. On the contrary, they are a natural result of any marriage. You can't hold your breath and avoid them or make them go away. But you can control how you handle stress and disagreements within your marriage.

First, it's important to remember that most stress is temporary. This is easier to see with those big life changes, where events happen on a specific date. But it's true with smaller stressful situations too. If you're going through a PCS move or a deployment, you are both going to be stressed for several months before and after that event. If you're struggling with unemployment or staying home to raise a baby or toddler, then life can feel messy and frustrating. This is a difficult season of your marriage. But it doesn't mean your marriage will always feel like this. You may be walking through a swampy valley right now, but that doesn't mean you'll never stand on a mountaintop or enjoy a beautiful sunrise. It's okay to muddle through this together for a while as you keep working toward the marriage you both want and deserve.

Next, consider that your spouse is going through some of the same stress you are. They may handle it in a different way, and they may have different methods of expressing their frustration, but ultimately this is a situation that you are going through together—as a couple. Don't distance yourself from your spouse when you are feeling overwhelmed. And don't make them into the enemy by blaming your situation on them or on the military. You are a family, and you're on the same team. Avoid the trap of comparing whose life is more difficult right now or who has a bigger "right" to be stressed and frustrated. You are both allowed to be stressed, but you must always work together to help each other instead of tearing each other down. When you are facing struggles in your military marriage, hold onto your spouse's hand (metaphorically if they are far away) and get through it together.

Remember to always focus on the roots of your marriage and keep the big picture in mind. It's easy to get distracted by, well, life. You are probably now quite aware of your partner's bad habits and every annoying habit they have. But that isn't why you married them! When your marriage needs a little encouragement, remind yourself why you got married in the first place. Was it because of your spouse's great smile and ability to stay calm when you were upset? Or perhaps their numerous kind words and deeds that demonstrate how much they love you? Because of the way they always support you and act like your biggest fan? Maybe because they always know how to make you laugh and brighten your darkest mood? For these reasons and a thousand others, you gave them your heart in marriage. This current stressful season won't last forever, but your love can last that long. When you are feeling frustrated, hold onto those precious tender memories. Look at old photos or read your previous love letters. Write down some of the positive qualities of your spouse that you love. Think about the big picture of your marriage—what you want your relationship to look like years from now, perhaps even after military service. Discuss these dreams and goals with your spouse. When you are both working toward a shared goal in the future, it can make the challenges you are facing right now a little bit easier to bear.

Finally, let's admit that many marriage challenges come down to the same issue: communication. If you and your spouse feel disconnected right now, there was probably some miscommunication along the way. This isn't necessarily one person's fault, and it won't get fixed by placing blame on each other. Instead, discuss ways you can both improve communication in the future. Is there a certain way they respond to your problems that really upsets you? Is there a habit they have or a chore they avoid that creates stress at home? Is something about your evening routines or sleep schedules getting in the way of intimacy? Do they have behaviors that cause you to worry about their faithfulness to your marriage? All these things can be worked out with the right amount of time and effort, but someone has to bring them up and take the first step. Communication issues won't get fixed overnight, but shining a light on them is necessary for any improvement. Always be gentle and non-confrontational when discussing relationship challenges. Remember, this situation is temporary, and you can work through it together. Keep the big picture in mind.

Everyone's marriage goes through rough patches and needs a little encouragement now and then. So try not to feel guilty or embarrassed that you and your spouse are in a difficult phase right now. You aren't alone in this struggle, and you don't have to find your way through it by yourself. Begin by improving communication with your spouse and trying the mental resets mentioned here. It can always be beneficial to discuss things with a trusted friend or a counselor too. You and your relationship just need a little encouragement to get through this difficult season. So here is a warm hug from me to you to help you through!

Changes of Address

My Story
When Does the Fun Begin?

I sat in a tiny unfamiliar rental car, trying to psych myself up for the challenge of driving through equally tiny and unfamiliar foreign streets. I didn't have much experience driving a stick shift—the only option from the Spanish car rental company—so I was learning on the fly. This little car was my only transportation from our hotel to the nearby military base, our new duty station in Rota, Spain. In the back seat, my three small children were crammed into three car seats. They fussed and whined, normal behavior for kids under age four who are way off their schedule and far away from everything familiar. I struggled to concentrate on driving—shifting gears, reading European road signs, and dodging pedestrians who wandered into the street.

That morning I was on an essential mission, taking care of the many details of arriving at a new duty station. Normally my husband, Dan, would take care of these tasks, but he was already at work. He arrived at his new unit on the same day as a major terror attack in Benghazi, Libya. Overnight, half the unit had mobilized and flown to Africa. Dan and others who remained behind were now working long shifts and sleeping in the office. He had to jump into his new position, with no time to adjust. No one had time to help him—or me—settle in.

So I dropped Dan off at his office and spent the day driving from place to place to complete paperwork. It was like some kind of horrible scavenger hunt, conducted in a mixture of Spanish and English, where I had to get three kids out of car seats at every location. I was exhausted before I started, jet-lagged, and tired of being stuck in cramped quarters with the kids. Getting out with them in the car was not much of an improvement, but we didn't know anyone who could watch them. We didn't know anyone in the whole country. I knew moving to Europe would be challenging, but this is not how I imagined our first few weeks would be.

Every move has its own challenges. With an overseas move, there is an extra layer of logistical obstacles and paperwork. For us, the addition of a major international incident ratcheted up the stress. But even a fairly straightforward move within the same state is a major change for the whole family. If you are preparing for a military move or going through one right now, you have probably researched the details. Maybe you have a checklist, even multiple checklists, and your plans are in place. But you may not be as prepared for the emotional exhaustion of moving. For us, the move to Spain was an extreme example, but we have experienced similar emotional upheavals in each of our moves.

I have learned what to expect, but the emotions aren't just boxes I can check off and put behind me. They are part of the adjustment process I have to walk through each time. The moving boxes can be unpacked and sorted in a matter of days, but unpacking the emotions of a move is a less tangible process. Sometimes it takes weeks, but more often it takes months, and it's a journey that can't be rushed or avoided.

The challenge of our move to Spain began when Dan was first selected for the assignment. First, he had to attend training and was away from home for weeks while I began the process of getting ready to move overseas. The kids and I had to go through a medical screening process. We applied for passports for everyone, even the baby. I put our house on the market and kept it ready for home tours, which could happen at the drop of a hat. I studied Spanish. We sold a vehicle. We tried to save money. It was a frustrating, whirlwind process. By the time we finally landed and got off the plane in Spain, my energy reserves were low, and the road ahead was still long. Then the news of the Benghazi attack added to Dan's rigorous work schedule.

To make matters worse, for our first few weeks in Spain, our friends and neighbors back home wanted us to send exciting news and "vacation" photos of all the fun we were having on our "exotic assignment." The pictures they had in mind did not match the reality of the life we were living right then.

Every day brought new challenges and tears of frustration. On numerous occasions, we got lost in foreign towns without a map or GPS. The simplest tasks like dialing a phone number or paying with cash were suddenly more complicated. Every time I tried to complete an errand, it seemed I went about it the wrong way and had to take three additional steps. Driving the kids around in that tiny stick-shift car, I missed our roomy minivan. We missed our own furniture and beds, which had not arrived yet with our household goods. We missed friends and family. I missed hearing my language. It was lonely and exhausting and not at all like a vacation. I realized getting used to a completely new way of life would take time.

Fortunately, as difficult as it can be, the frustration of moving doesn't last forever. It took us a while to learn our way around and feel comfortable on our new base. Eventually, during our second or third month in Spain, we started to relax. We finally had our minivan and household goods, which helped us feel more at home. We learned our way around town and found a favorite restaurant. Our finances began to level out, allowing us to plan our first big family trip. I got the kids enrolled in preschool. I made new friends. We attended local parades and festivals and finally got a taste of Spanish culture. Life was different, but it gradually began to feel wonderful again.

I have experienced this cycle again and again, with every move. I know it's hard to move your life and your family to a new place, no matter how near or far. I've been there, a stranger in a new neighborhood or another country, wondering how in the world I was going to make the most of this place.

Our family has experienced many moves. Sometimes we've packed and moved ourselves. Other times we had professional movers. We've relocated overseas, across country, and across town. Most of the time we planned weeks or months ahead of time. Each move had its own unique challenges. One time, we packed and moved our whole household, including four kids and two pets, in ten days. In 2020, we moved ourselves across country during the COVID pandemic and were immediately greeted by a hurricane.

Speaking from the other side of all these moving experiences, I can tell you this: The new friends and experiences and memories are worth the effort and readjustment. The tears of frustration will eventually be replaced with smiles. Don't push yourself too hard or expect too much too soon. There's really no way to skip the hard part, but it does get easier. In the end, I hope you will discover all the richness and joy of your mobile military life.

Open When
You're Making Your
First Military Move

Dear Relocating Friend,

Before you began military life, you probably heard there could be a lot of moving around. Maybe you've been dreading having to relocate, or maybe you are looking forward to seeing new places and meeting new people.

It's normal to be nervous and uncertain about your first military move. Maybe this is the first big move of your life, possibly your first time living far from extended family. I can't promise it will be a smooth process, but you can manage this task and survive. With thousands of military families moving every year, you won't be alone.

How often you move and where you go depends on your service member's career field. The locations for some jobs are limited to a handful of installations, while others are not. When a military member receives orders to move to a new location, it's called a permanent change of station, or PCS. It's common for military members and their families to move every two to four years, though you may have shorter or longer assignments.

When the military requires a service member to move from one duty station or military installation to another in a PCS move, the names of the service member's dependents authorized to move with them are listed on the official paperwork, or PCS orders. The government covers the cost of travel for relocating the military member and those dependents, as well as transporting their belongings to the new location.

This means a moving company will pack, load, and transport your belongings, up to a certain weight limit determined by rank, family size, and your assignment location. You may also choose a do-it-yourself move, commonly known as a DITY move, or personally procured move (PPM), instead of using a moving company. In this case, the military will reimburse certain expenses. Either way, if your shipment exceeds the weight limit, you will have to cover the cost of the overage.

Sometimes you may have an idea of when or where you are moving—sometimes both, sometimes one or the other—even before your service member is officially notified. Generally, your service member should receive notification and orders at least thirty days before a move.

Very likely, the question of where you will go is a big deal to you. It is for all of us. The acronym CONUS designates moves inside the continental United States. The acronym OCONUS describes any move outside the continental US. Military members, and by extension their families, have some input into where they would like to move. Perhaps your service member has told you some of the most likely locations, based on their service branch, specific job, and rank. But these are usually more like educated guesses. The military is famous for sending people to unexpected places, even though service members may give input on official paperwork fondly called a "dream sheet." Ultimately, the needs of the military and the mission determine where your military member is assigned, though documented family needs and issues may also be part of the equation.

If your service member has a reason to request a particular duty station, for instance if they have partial custody of a child in a certain state, or if you or one of your children needs medical care available in a particular location, special requests for assignments are given due consideration.

Waiting to learn where you are going to live can be an excruciating process. Sometimes it feels like you are holding your breath and everything is paused while you wait for an answer. Other times, you may feel like time is going way too quickly, and you are caught up in a whirlwind of packing and to-do lists. It can certainly be a confusing process, and it doesn't help when most of your service member's explanations involve more acronyms. Just keep asking questions and looking up moving resources. Remember that your service member isn't dragging you through this PCS process as a punishment. It is a challenge that you must face together and conquer as a team.

Typically, your military member will have an idea when they will receive their next orders based on when their current orders expire. Occasionally, they will have the option to extend their current orders for one or more years and remain in the same location. If your service member is attending a training course or military school, they may know they will leave when training is done but may not know where they will be assigned until graduation.

When your service member has official PCS orders in hand for a specific location, then you can begin to schedule your moving and travel dates. Yay! This is the time for your research to shine, as you finally start making decisions and filing paperwork. Nothing is final until those orders are in hand, giving your service member the authority to schedule movers, get plane tickets, clear medical records, and other actions necessary for a move. That's when you know for sure this is really happening. Be aware, however, it's possible for orders to change at the last minute, even after they are official. As I've said before, military life requires us to be flexible.

Hang on, because it could be a wild ride; and it could also be an extraordinary adventure. Either way, you won't be alone.

Open When
You Want to Plan a Smooth Move

Dear Moving Planner,

It's time to get ready to move. Maybe you love to make lists and feel organized; or maybe you feel like a hot mess and you just want to get control of this hectic process and the emotions that go with it! Whichever one applies, this is the letter for you.

No matter where you are going, near or far, the logistics of moving are a lot to take in. When you have to make decisions and operate on someone else's timeline—which, let's face it, describes most of military life—the result is stress and conflict. You and your spouse may have insignificant disagreements during a move because there is so much going on, and you are both tired and over it.

Sound familiar? Then read on, my friend. You are not the first person to feel overwhelmed when the military tells you to uproot your whole life. Each move requires plans and preparations tailored to the situation. Experience teaches military spouses to remain flexible and ready to accommodate delays and last-minute changes.

The best way to feel calmer and in more control of your move, even when you don't know all the details, is to plan ahead. Every move is different, but there are some similarities and common tasks each time. One way to help your move go more smoothly is to streamline your belongings. Being organized when you move out will help you get settled more quickly when you move into your new place. Even before you receive orders, you can start cleaning out closets, getting rid of outgrown clothes or unneeded items.

When your service member has orders, they can take a class to review the paperwork and details of the move. If you are allowed to attend, it's a good idea to go and learn all you can about the process. If you can't attend with your service member, the family support center has moving resources and can answer your questions as well.

Moving means a lot of paperwork. Keep it all together by creating a binder for all your to-do lists and moving documents, as well as other key paperwork. Your binder should include copies of your permanent change of station (PCS) orders and instructions, as well as legal documents such as your marriage license, birth certificates, passports, and car titles. Your binder might include individual folders for specific needs, such as school records and documents needed for enrollment. As you go through your move, add documents to your binder, including your travel receipts. In any move, always hand carry all your most important papers. Keep them in a safe place and be sure they don't get packed up with your household goods.

Your early planning may also include researching the new location to inform your decision about where to live: neighborhoods, housing costs, commute time, job opportunities, and school choices. Ask other military spouses or families what they know about your location to get a personal view. You will hear good and bad, so take opinions with a grain of salt, and get more than one person's perspective.

Moving requires you to make major decisions, sometimes one right after the other. One of the first big choices is determining which style of move you will do. You will have a choice to either let the military pay for a moving company to pack up and transport your household goods or to make the move yourself and be reimbursed for it. During peak season for military moves, usually spring and summer, if you are using professional movers, available dates may be limited.

Another way you can plan is by setting aside money in your savings for moving expenses. You can do this anytime, since your next move is often only a year or two away. Even though the military covers or reimburses most of your expenses, moving is costly, so it's a good idea to prepare. Some expenses have to be paid up front, and these add up: closing out your bills at one location, paying security deposits at the new location, buying or shipping a vehicle, setting up utilities, and more. Your military member will receive a moving or dislocation allowance to cover some of these expenses, but you should save receipts to file for reimbursement if needed after the move. Your service member can also request some of their moving allowance ahead of time to help cover expenses until they are reimbursed. Be aware pay advances must be paid back and will eventually be deducted from the service member's salary.

Some moving costs are unexpected or hidden. When you move, you must replace food and liquids, chemicals, and anything that can't be transported. This often means many of your beauty and craft items, cleaning supplies, as well as fuel or paint. Buying everything again at the next location can be pricey. Your moving company or the transportation office can tell you what items cannot be included in your shipment. The military will reimburse you for items damaged or broken during your move, but you will sometimes find the reimbursement doesn't cover all replacement or repairs. When you get to your new place, you may also need new rugs, window treatments, shelving, appliances, or furniture.

With a military move—as with all of military life—it helps to be prepared, patient, and flexible. Even when you're prepared, you can't plan for every possibility. Inevitably, something will change suddenly or go wrong. This is where patience and flexibility come in. A sense of humor helps too. Try to laugh with your spouse and adjust through the changes. Remember you are a team and the two of you are going to get through this together!

Open When
You Get Orders You Don't Want

Dear Disappointed Friend,

Let's be real here: not all military assignments are glamorous. Sometimes your loved one gets an assignment in the middle of nowhere or on the other side of the world. It can be a real punch in the gut. You may find yourself crying, despondent, or feeling out of control, wondering how this giant change is going to work in the life, marriage, and family you have worked hard to create.

It's okay to be disappointed you didn't get the assignment you wanted and mad at the military for making this so hard on you. It's normal to be upset about undesirable orders, because no matter what you do it is going to have a huge impact on your life. Let yourself feel everything you need to feel, and then let's talk through some of the options and see what might work for you.

Of course, you want to live with your spouse, but you may not want to live where the military is sending them. Maybe you've only heard bad news: military housing is old, and the schools are terrible, and it's in the middle of nowhere! No matter what you've heard or how bad you think the duty station location might be, I encourage you to give it a chance.

Most military spouses will tell you every assignment is as good as you make it. Sometimes the places we might consider the worst assignments are the places where military communities are strongest. People tend to bond in adversity, and you may make the best friends of your life or have a great group of neighbors in a "lousy location." Truly, you never know what treasures a community holds until you move there and give it a chance. No matter where you live, you can enjoy quality time with your family. Maybe there's not much to do around town, but you might find time to pursue a degree online, make a career change, or invest in your personal health and interests.

If you are disappointed about the new duty station because of the distance from your family, then take heart. Most military families end up living far from their parents and extended families. It's natural to spend some time mourning the celebrations you'll miss and the holidays you will spend apart. But in the modern age, living far from home doesn't need to change your relationship with your family. Technology makes it possible to stay connected at any distance. Whenever you are feeling far from your best friend or from your family, there are so many apps and social media options that can bridge that distance to help you feel closer. Plane tickets are increasingly affordable, so you can always plan a trip home or a visit from someone you love. You'll find that the military community can also become like a secondary family, with creative solutions to celebrating holidays and taking care of each other. This becomes more noticeable at the smaller duty stations, where military families come together and lean on each other for support.

Even if you are dragging your feet right now, approach the new assignment with an open mind. Yes, it's going to be a big change. Yes, it may challenge you or frustrate you. But there are many spouses who went kicking and screaming to an assignment, only to fall in love with it and then hate to leave. I can't explain how it happens, but it does. I do know it won't ever happen if you don't give this new place a chance. You are strong, and even if you don't want to hear it right now, you are incredibly resilient. You can find a way to bloom where you are planted. You can make the most of any place and create good memories with your service member.

Open When
You May Have to Live Apart

Dear One Facing Time Apart,

In military life you will sometimes be called upon to spend time away from your spouse, and deployment is not the only reason. Most often your time apart is chosen for you, but sometimes you may have to make hard decisions and choose it for yourself. Looks like you may be facing one or the other of these situations right now.

Maybe your service member has unaccompanied orders, an assignment that doesn't include family members for one reason or another. A service member might get unaccompanied orders to an overseas assignment that is less than two years or to a stateside assignment less than one year, perhaps for training. Families may also be excluded from the service member's orders if one or more have special medical needs that cannot be met at the new location. It's possible to appeal unaccompanied orders and request a change. Sometimes the military will work with your service member to include dependents on orders or to change the orders.

However, if the military decides not to change the orders, your service member will have to follow them. You do have a choice, though. You might choose to move to the new location on your own. If you do, you will be responsible for your moving and travel costs, as well as living expenses. This becomes much more complicated and expensive for an overseas location. If you are not included in the orders, you won't have command sponsorship, meaning you will not be guaranteed access to the military installation for healthcare or the use of other military facilities and benefits at that location. In case of any emergency, natural disaster, or political upheaval, this could put you in a precarious position.

Or perhaps you're on the flip side with another tough situation. Your service member has orders that do include you, but you are considering living apart from your spouse instead of making the move. In the military community, this is known as geographic-bachelor status, often called simply geo-baching. It might be because your service member already has orders to deploy right after they get to the new location. Maybe a move right now is not a good career decision for you or would be disruptive to your child's education, or you may have other circumstances that make living apart a viable solution.

Whatever the reason, when considering a geo-bach, be sure you have all facts and figures. Plan out the budget for your dual households that includes travel costs and any living expenses not covered by the military. Military families who choose to live apart have to bear the cost of maintaining two households, as well as any travel back and forth. The military does not provide additional income or travel pay. Your service member will receive their housing allowance based on their assigned duty location. If the family staying behind lives in military housing, they may have to move out. Geo-baching is a big decision and not one to take lightly. Separating your family is costly in more ways than one, and you should only choose it if it's the best option for long-term reasons and for the entire family.

Whether you are facing time apart because of an unaccompanied assignment or geo-bachelor status, you and your service member need to maintain strong and positive communication. If your location allows you to be together for a few days each week or each month, be aware that your family dynamic will change each time. You will be one unit operating out of two locations. Make major decisions together, but respect one another's space and smaller, personal decisions. Plan vacation or time away together as well as time at home together. If you have kids, get on the same page with parenting, as much as possible, and keep the same rules whether both parents are present or only one. If you find yourself often at odds about minor concerns when you're together, look for the real source of the conflict and try to resolve it. Always remember your love and trust for one another. You will get through this and be together again.

Make sure you and your service member discuss how you will communicate and support each other across the distance when you are apart. Maintain your own support network of friends around you who will help you stay connected and grounded. Otherwise, you may feel out of the loop without your service member to connect you to all that's going on in your military community or on the installation. Spend time investing in yourself while your service member is not with you. Self-care is always worthwhile.

The military doesn't always surprise us with good orders. Sometimes news about a move is not what we want to hear. When you know the options, you will know better how to make an informed decision and make the most of a difficult situation.

As a military spouse, when the military gives you lemons sometimes you make lemonade. When you have to figure out how to live in two places at once, you might have to figure out a way to turn those lemons into a darn good margarita!

Open When
You Get Orders to Move Overseas

Dear World Traveler,

Congratulations on your overseas orders! This is the assignment most military families dream of. You may have already experienced some of the envy your friends feel when you tell them where you are going. But I know on the inside, even if you are excited, you are also freaking out about everything ahead of you. Uprooting your family and transporting your life to another country is a big deal and a big job. You have to sort out what to put in storage, what to take, and how your belongings will get there. You also may be a little nervous about being an ocean away from home, or how you will figure out shopping, driving, and living in another country.

Moving overseas is a giant undertaking and requires careful planning. It will be less overwhelming when you break it down into essential tasks and handle them one at a time.

When you know your moving date, you can begin to work with your spouse to determine what needs to happen, when, and who will be responsible for each step or task. Some paperwork only your service member can complete. Some tasks you'll have to do together, and others you can divide and conquer.

Mapping out the steps might help you feel a little bit more in control of this stressful move, so here are a few steps to get started.

Medical screenings will include a physical and dental check-up and immunizations for everyone in the family. Some locations require additional immunizations, and all routine shots must be up to date. The military wants to be sure the overseas location can accommodate medical needs, including any medications, treatments, or therapies.

Each member of the family will most likely need a passport. As military families moving overseas, you are eligible for no-fee passports, processed through your military installation travel office.

These passports authorize military families to travel to and from and live in a host nation under a Status of Forces Agreement (SOFA) between the US and the host nation. Your no-fee passports will each include a SOFA stamp indicating your status. No-fee passports are not for personal travel while you are overseas. To take advantage of travel opportunities, obtain regular civilian passports too. You need to apply and pay for these on your own.

When moving overseas, your military member should request a sponsor. The sponsor is a service member—typically in your spouse's receiving unit—who's familiar with the duty station and will help with your transition before and after you arrive. A sponsor can arrange a rental car and billeting for you and may offer to pick you up from the airport when you arrive in country. A sponsor can be a valuable resource for your move, answering questions about housing, schools, and more about life in your new location. Don't assume your sponsor will take care of everything. Ask for guidance and help, and they will likely be willing to help in any way they can and let you know what steps you need to take for your own transition.

When moving overseas, you may have as many as three separate shipments within your weight allowance. The first is your household goods, which will likely include the bulk of your belongings. This shipment travels by sea and may take two or three months to arrive. Your express shipment travels by air and should be scheduled to arrive soon after you do. This shipment should include immediate necessities, such as clothes, electronics, cooking utensils, baby equipment, bikes, and other items you will need during your first month overseas. It's a good idea to include school supplies for your kids in this shipment too. The final shipment is for items you want to keep but don't want to take overseas. These will be professionally packed and transferred to storage. For example, your appliances may not be compatible at some locations. Or you may anticipate limited living space and decide to leave large furniture behind. The transportation office or your sponsor can give you details about what you are authorized to take or advised to store.

The government will ship one vehicle per service member free of charge. Get information ahead of time and be prepared to follow very strict shipping requirements when you take your vehicle to the port. Your car will take a couple of months to arrive, so you'll probably want a rental until then. Ask your sponsor if you need an international driver's license to be able to rent a car upon arrival. If so, be sure to get one before you leave the US. If you need a second car, you may want to purchase a used vehicle when you arrive overseas. Because departing military members often sell vehicles on the way out, there's usually a selection of cars available on the military "lemon lot." Within a few weeks of your arrival, you will need to take a test for an official driver's license in country, another thing to ask your sponsor about.

Your dog or cat can move overseas with you, but the military does not pay or reimburse any fees for shipping animals. If you want your pet to move with you, start planning—and saving—soon. Transporting pets overseas can be pricey. Check with the airline for their travel requirements (health certificate, microchip) and the host nation for their requirements or limitations (number, certain breeds). Pets other than dogs or cats are usually not allowed to travel overseas at all.

With an overseas move, you will spend some time in a hotel or temporary housing, living out of a suitcase. Pack wisely, considering the weather and your weight limit. Include a few favorite toys and games for the kids. Hand carry small valuables, such as jewelry, personal electronics, and your binder with all your important paperwork.

Each part of an overseas move comes with many small but not minor details. In addition, you will need to do all the same preparation you do for any move, cleaning out closets, preparing documents to hand carry as you travel, researching housing options, and more.

You might also consider taking a language course to become familiar with your host country's language. For the most part, you will be able to get by with English, but it's nice to know a few key phrases. When you arrive at your new location, you can also ask about language and culture classes to help you learn how to navigate and enjoy your new home.

It's a lot to think about. An overseas move is a process that takes months of planning. You may be stressed and worried for a while.

Right now, when people comment enviously about how lucky you are to be going overseas, you might feel frustrated and annoyed. They have no idea how much weight is on your shoulders as you prepare to move to and live in another country.

Look forward to the time when you will look around at your new surroundings and soak in the amazing fact that you are living overseas. You will get there! You'll find cultural opportunities, new holidays to celebrate, delicious food to eat, and exciting places to travel. You just need to jump through some hoops and take care of these tasks first. Make your to-do list, choose one chore to tackle today, and start the journey toward your overseas adventure!

Open When
It's Time to Clean Out All the Stuff

Dear Owner of All the Stuff,

Your moving date is approaching, and your house is a mess! When you look around, all you see are full closets, cabinets, and drawers. It is certainly difficult to imagine everything neatly packed and stacked into moving boxes. Yet one way or another, you know you need to start going through things. The task can feel daunting, and it's difficult to decide where to begin.

In a way, the military forces you to spring clean when you move, because they assign your family a specific weight limit for moving or storing household goods. Most families find their moving weight allowance covers their needs, but anything over that amount can result in hefty out-of-pocket costs. An easy way to get comfortably below your weight limit is to clean out excess stuff you no longer need. You don't want to hang on to everything, but then you also don't want to get rid of too much only to need replacements at the next duty station.

Every military move, whether stateside or overseas sparks a re-evaluation of your life choices and purchases. You start to look at all of your belongings differently. You might find yourself wondering, *Do I really need all of this?* or *How can we comfortably live without that?*

There isn't a supreme right or wrong answer about what to keep and what to get rid of, but lightening your load is a good idea. More than likely, you have things you no longer use or need, and it will simplify your life and your move to get rid of them before the packers come. You don't have to become an extreme minimalist, but it is definitely worthwhile to clean out your closets and start fresh at the next location.

When you look around at your messy garage or overflowing closets, the idea of cleaning out your home may feel overwhelming. It's a heavy burden to pile on your shoulders, especially when you are facing all the other stressful details of a PCS. Just approach this daunting job one thing at a time. Find a way to break down each task. Maybe room-by-room works best for you, or perhaps you want to start with closets first. If you stay focused on your plan, you will see results. Writing down your tasks and checking them off can help you stay focused and monitor your progress. Stick with one task at a time in the room, closet, or shelf you are working on. Sort items to be kept or tossed. Put away misplaced items so they will be packed with the room where they belong.

It can be hard to decide what you should throw away. Start by getting rid of broken items. No one needs those. Then, go through the house and decide what you no longer need. Can you jettison clothes or toys the kids have outgrown? The DVD collection that's only collecting dust? You can donate or consign these items to your military thrift store or have a garage sale, either real or virtual. Which you choose depends on whether your priority is saving time or making a few bucks.

If you have children, you might want to do some of the clearing out without them, because any toy can seem like a treasure to them in the moment, even a broken one that's been forgotten in the back of the closet—until now. Be sensitive in these situations. A big reaction to a particular toy may really be a reaction to the upcoming move. Give kids some decision-making power over toys they want to keep. They do need a sense of security and continuity, knowing they will see their favorite things again when they get to their new home.

If your children are old enough, let them sort out their own toys to sell or donate—maybe after you have tossed the broken ones. They may appreciate earning some money or the good feeling of giving a toy or book to someone else who will enjoy it.

You will discover a familiar cycle in military life. While some military families are cleaning out and getting rid of bulky items to move out, others are moving in and finding out what they need in their new place. This is good news for you. You can sell or give away things you don't need before you move, and you will likely find a ready source of new-to-you items when you get to your destination.

Knowing ahead of time what you can or can't take with you will make some of your decisions easier. The transportation office has information about regulations and restrictions. If you're moving overseas, ask about any limitations on large furniture and appliances, as well as any other household items. Moving companies will not transport hazardous materials, such as paint, cleaning chemicals, automotive oil, propane, or aerosol cans. Follow your local laws to dispose of these items properly or give them away.

Evaluate your furniture to determine what pieces might be too delicate or worn out to survive the move, or too large to fit in the next house. If you are moving overseas and will not be taking large furniture or appliances, decide whether to get rid of them or put them in storage, depending on age or condition. Consider how they will tolerate storage. If you are moving overseas, you might wish to put family heirlooms or furniture in storage rather than moving them across the ocean.

As you begin to tackle the task of sorting through everything you own, make a plan and a reasonable schedule. You didn't acquire all this stuff in a day, so you probably won't be able to sort it all out in a day either. Give yourself some grace. It is an emotional task to examine and evaluate all your possessions.

If this process causes conflict with your spouse, avoid making it a lose-lose proposition. Think through together how often items really get used, and always consider compromise. Something that is not meaningful to you might have meaning for your spouse and vice-versa. Your most treasured belongings are your spouse and your family, so be kind to each other and face this challenge together!

As you go through your things, don't forget to take a walk down memory lane every now and then. Memorabilia from high school, your first date, even your wedding day, or your babies will always be treasured, but not every item has to be preserved. If it's not practical to keep something, find a way to savor the memory it holds. Take photos, perhaps. Honoring the memory will help you feel more peaceful about parting with belongings and mementos you associate with happy times.

Cleaning out your home before a move is a big job! Yes, this is going to be a difficult time, but you will get through it. Once you get started, just keep moving forward. The sooner you start and get it done, the more prepared you will be for your move!

Open When
Your Orders Change on Short Notice

Dear Rushed Friend,

Usually, the military will give you several months of notice before you have to make a permanent change of station. This means you know where you're going and have time to prepare your belongings, look for housing, research schools, and make all the necessary arrangements. But by now, you've probably realized that the military doesn't always operate in the most convenient way for you. And this time, they are forcing you to move much quicker than you had planned.

Sometimes it's not the military's fault. Maybe your service member had to complete a school or training assignment before their orders could become official. In that case, it's normal not to find out about the new orders until the week of graduation. You may not know where you are going, but you are fairly certain a move is in your very near future.

Other times, orders change at the last minute. Maybe your service member thought everything was set for them to go to a particular location. But then the unforeseen happened, and suddenly you are looking at moving somewhere completely different.

And then there are times when a promotion comes with a bonus move. Congratulations, maybe? Whether or not your service member expected this promotion, the celebration will mean big changes for the whole family when a move is part of the deal.

One way or another, you are moving very soon. Ready or not, here it comes, and you may not feel ready at all. When you look around, your house seems filled with an incredible amount of stuff. How can you possibly get all of it prepared for a move to the new location, perhaps including kids and pets? And then there's the matter of your job if you have to leave it. Will you be able to find a job at your new location on such short notice? Every time you sit down to tackle one task, your entire to-do list crowds into your thoughts. Sometimes a whirlwind move feels like a carnival ride—the horrible, spinning kind that makes you sick to your stomach.

If this move has you spinning, then take a moment. Slow down your whirling thoughts. You are going to get through this. It might be messy and rushed and not your first choice, but you are going to figure this out, one step at a time.

The first obstacle you might run into on a short-notice move is not having enough time to request government movers. Professional moving companies are usually booked weeks in advance. If you need to move quickly—at least for a stateside move—you may have to manage the move by yourself. You can choose to do the work yourself or you may be able to hire a moving company independently and be reimbursed for the cost. Check with your transportation office, because advance approval is required for a full reimbursement.

As you make your short notice plans, talk to your spouse and map out the biggest priorities between now and moving day. Divide up errands and tasks to make sure the essentials get done. Instead of getting distracted or overwhelmed, break down the process to the essential tasks.

Sort out housing at the new location. If you plan to live in military housing, contact the housing office at your receiving installation immediately to learn your options and get on a waiting list. Otherwise, start looking at properties to buy or rent, and contact a real estate agent. If you won't have somewhere to move by moving day, talk to the receiving installation about temporary housing options like local hotels or rentals on base.

If you have children, research the schools in the area, contact the receiving school(s), and initiate an application for enrollment, online if possible.

Visit your doctors and dentist and request hard copies of your patient records. If you have been going to military hospitals, these records should transfer to the next location, but having printed or downloaded copies is a great backup in case there is a delay in accessing those records.

If necessary, put in notice at your current job and start looking for new work. With all the pressure of the quick move, you may have to put the job search on the back burner for a short time while you take care of other things. At least browse opportunities in the area and update your resume to be prepared when the time comes.

Clean out the house. You don't need to move everything with you to the new location. Maybe it's time to get rid of some old furniture or the baby clothes stacked in the garage. Purge as you go, so you don't waste time packing what you don't need. You may not have time to offer anything for sale, but you can donate or consign it to a thrift store.

Plan time to say goodbye. Even though your departure is rushed, you still deserve to say goodbye to friends and coworkers. It may sound like just one more thing to add to your busy schedule right now, but ultimately it will give you a sense of peace and closure. If you have kids, this is an important step for them too. Don't skip it.

Ask for help. Your friends will most likely be glad to pitch in—especially military friends who have been through plenty of moving situations. Make a list and divide it up. Extra hands will help you complete many tasks in a short amount of time. It's also an opportunity to spend time with your friends before you leave.

Yes, this is a lot to get done in a short time, but if you focus on these essential tasks, your move will go quickly and more smoothly. You may feel rushed and exhausted, but try not to take it out on your service member. Instead of fighting, focus on the big picture and the essential tasks. If you can take care of those, everything else will fall into place. You can take time to do more research and adjust to your new place after you get there.

I can feel your frustration, but I encourage you to focus on the timeline as it moves forward. Very soon you will be on the other side of the moving process, unpacking boxes at your new home! Think how proud you will be when you get to start unpacking at the new place. Stay focused on the goal and do your best. That's all anyone can ask of you right now. You are strong, and you can get through this.

Open When

You're Thinking About a DITY Move

Dear Motivated Mover,

When military families choose to move themselves, it's often referred to as a do-it-yourself, or DITY, move, but it is officially known as a personally procured move, or PPM. These are usually only authorized for stateside moves.

For any move required by the military, the government covers the cost of relocation for everyone listed on the permanent change of station (PCS) orders. A weight limit is established, based on your service member's rank, your family size, and sometimes the location. Within those limits, the cost of your move is covered, whether you do it yourself or use a military-approved moving company.

If you choose the latter, your moving dates are scheduled through the transportation office at your installation. Professional movers come to your house, pack up everything, put it on a truck, and transport it all to your home at your next duty station. Your shipment may spend some time in storage en route if necessary. When your shipment arrives at your new home, more professional movers will deliver and unload it. If anything is damaged, the military contract with the moving company covers payment for repair or replacement.

In a DITY move, the government will pay you a large percentage of what a professional move would cost for your household. You can use these funds as you choose—to rent a moving truck, purchase packing materials, or even hire your own movers. Doing the majority of packing and moving on your own is hard work, but it allows you to make money while moving yourself.

If you are considering a DITY move, first figure out how much you could earn based on your weight allowance, taking into account the cost of packing materials, transportation, fuel, and other expenses. Is it enough to make the hard work worthwhile? Do you have enough time, manpower, or friends to help you move?

Sometimes the benefits of letting the military move you may outweigh the financial benefit of a DITY move. If you have very young children and no one to help, you may not have enough free hands or time to spend packing boxes. If you are moving without your service member for some reason—it happens—it might not be worth the stress of managing the entire move yourself. If you would have to take unpaid time off work to do the packing, then the compensation may not be worth it. Weigh the options and decide what works for you. The circumstances will be different with each move.

Making money for a move is a nice perk, but you will work hard to earn it. It's time-consuming and exhausting. There is also the risk of damage, which is not covered if you move yourself. You are responsible for everything. If you drop a TV, smash the box with your Christmas ornaments, or lose the hardware to assemble your bed, you bear the cost and the consequences.

Another option is to move some of your belongings yourself, even if a professional moving company handles the bulk of your household goods. This is known as a partial DITY. You might want to pack and transport irreplaceable valuables, heirloom furniture, photos, or simply the necessities you'll need right away at your new location. As long as you are within your weight allowance, you can get paid for what you transport on your own, even if it's only a small part of what you are moving.

If you and your service member decide to move yourselves, either fully or partially, make sure you're both completely on board with the decision. Again, it's hard work. You'll get sweaty and sore. Tempers are likely to flare. Stick together as a team, and don't blame one another when things go wrong.

Good organization is always helpful when you move, and it's essential when you move yourself. Create a folder or binder to keep all your moving paperwork and documentation in one place, as you would with any move. For a DITY or a partial DITY move, you'll need to document your moving costs, so hang on to all your receipts. You will need to present these records to be reimbursed for your expenses.

Moving costs include the cost of renting a truck, packing materials, gas, meals, and hotel costs. Keep all records of moving costs in your binder, along with copies of orders, birth certificates, and other important documents.

Plan a timeline for your move and set goals for completing each task. Start earlier than you think you will need to. Don't save all the tasks for the final week. Your service member will also have to complete check-out procedures at work before departure, and their professional to-do list is every bit as essential as the task list at home. Discuss priorities. Divide and conquer. Share the challenges to avoid unnecessary conflict over the process.

Estimate how many boxes you need to pack each room and the number of days set aside for packing. Set a goal of a certain number of boxes or rooms to pack each day. Sure, you may spend some late nights wrapping up dishes, but it really is possible to pack up your entire house in a few days if you focus on that task.

When you choose to move yourself, it is worthwhile to invest in packing supplies. Yes, you may be able to get free moving boxes from a neighbor or from a local warehouse, but they will be of random sizes and could be damaged already. Used boxes may work for some items, but not all. Getting professional-grade supplies means the boxes are modular, designed to stack and fit together in a moving truck and to fit a variety of household items. You can purchase boxes especially for lamps, vacuums, and electronics. Original boxes are usually the best way to protect delicate and expensive items such as computers and televisions, so it's a good idea to hang on to those for all your moves.

Boxes designed especially for china or glassware are reinforced to protect delicate items. Furniture pads and professional-grade plastic wrap can help protect furniture from scratches. Bubble wrap will be essential for anything delicate or breakable. Having the right materials will make your packing process go faster and help your belongings arrive in good condition. Take the time to research professional tricks and hacks for packing and moving.

Before moving day, don't forget to round up some help for the heavy lifting. If the kids are too young to help, ask a friend to watch them for the day so they won't be in the way or get hurt. Maybe you have friends who are willing to work in exchange for dinner, or you may want to hire some help. If you are driving the moving truck, consider inviting another friend or family member to drive your personal vehicles and follow behind, so you can stay with the moving truck at all times.

Whatever you use to transport your shipment—a moving truck, personal vehicle, trailer, or a storage container—you'll need to weigh it when it is empty and then again after you have loaded it. The military requires both weight receipts to calculate your reimbursement, so be sure the weight documentation goes in your binder.

Moving yourself can be a lot of work, but with good planning it can be well worthwhile. Weigh the pros and cons and discuss it with your service member. If you find a way to make it work, it's a memorable experience that can really pay off in the end!

Open When

You Say Goodbye to a Home You Love

Dear Moving Friend,

It's almost time to stand at the threshold of this house with tears in your eyes and take one last look behind you before you walk out the door. It won't be easy.

You have great things ahead of you, but good memories are hard to leave behind. Even with a new, exciting future ahead, the moment is still bittersweet. Saying goodbye to a home you've loved is hard, whether you're leaving your childhood home, the first home you lived in with your military loved one, or the place where you brought home a newborn—or two. You may feel you are leaving so many memories behind: lonely rooms during deployment, the floors you walked with a fussy baby, the kitchen where you made holiday meals together. You filled your home with friends, good food, used furniture, and laughter. You made this house a home. But when all your belongings are packed up and moved out, it's just a house again, an empty shell with echoes of memories the next resident won't even hear.

It's okay to cry when you leave part of your life behind. At many duty stations, you will leave a house with no expectation of returning. Even if you're leaving a house you own, one you will keep and rent to others, there's no guarantee you will be stationed there again. If you do return in a few years, after more children or other life changes, this house might no longer be a good fit for you. Closing and locking the door that final time is truly the end of a certain chapter of your life. No matter what happens, you can't relive those days again.

Here's what you can do: treasure the memories and walk forward. Before you go, before the movers pack up your belongings, make sure to treasure some memories. Save something physical, like photos, videos, or souvenirs, so you—and perhaps your children—can enjoy those memories for years to come. Savor the memory of this chapter and prepare to close the door. When you know you have captured the joy of a place, it makes it easier to leave. The memories are about the people, not the place. A house is only a house, but your spouse is home. No matter where you move, you will find home with the one you love.

Everything hard can be done one step at a time, including stepping out the door for the last time. Clean out closets. Pack up the curtains. Once your belongings are packed, it's easier to see that even when you leave this house behind, you will take the memories with you. Keep telling the story of that tiny kitchen, or the creaking door, or the time you painted the wall the wrong color.

Then step into your next empty house and realize its potential. The next house is not full of memories yet, but it soon will be. First, fill it with the pictures and souvenirs and memories of your old house. And then watch as you start to have new adventures and new stories to tell in this one. One day, the empty house you just moved into will feel like a home too.

Open When
Your Kids Don't Want to Move

Dear Parent Taking All the Blame,

You had to break the news about the move to the kids, and it didn't go well. Maybe this will be their first move, and they are sad and confused. Or maybe your child has made many moves. They have a school and friends they love, and they've decided to dig in their heels and resist this news. Moving the whole family because of one person's job may seem unfair to you or your children. You may be feeling overwhelmed with guilt and trying to figure out the gentlest way to get your kids through this ordeal.

Even children as young as one year can be affected by a move. They will be separated from friends and possibly family. If they are a bit older, they will have to change schools and learn a whole new cast of teachers, rules, and routines. You may fear they will miss out on opportunities, sports teams, or competitions they've been working for and looking forward to. No, it's not easy, and it's not fair. Your children didn't ask to be born into this military life, and maybe you don't blame them for throwing a fit when they get hit with the bad news.

Yes, you may have to get through some tough times while moving with your kids, but ultimately, military life has many positives. You are giving them new experiences and helping them to become stronger. Don't be too hard on yourself or wallow in parenting guilt. Despite their tears now, your children will adjust to your new home, and most likely even enjoy it. Someday they may even thank you for the moving experience. But be prepared to wait a while for that!

Adults who grew up as military kids—although they may have complained about moving at the time—say their many transitions gave them valuable skills and experiences. They learned to adapt and make new friends quickly. They gained empathy for others, and they experienced new parts of the country and the world they wouldn't have seen otherwise.

So how can you fast-forward through the current tears and tantrums to a more positive outcome? While you can't avoid the pain of moving and saying goodbye, you can take steps to help your child through the sadness. If they are young, look for books and videos made to help military kids with moving. It will help them understand and talk through their emotions about moving. Loss comes with grief. Let them express their grief, even if you get tired of hearing about it.

Don't sugar-coat the challenges or dismiss their feelings, but also don't treat this or any move as a tragedy. Be open with your child and admit moving will be difficult for the whole family. At the same time, keep a positive outlook and sense of adventure. Your good attitude and loving support will help them, even if they are reluctant.

You can talk about the benefits of the next duty station but wait until your child is receptive. If you start telling them the positives of the new place when they are not ready to hear it, they may become angry or believe you don't care about or understand their feelings. Don't take it personally if they take out their frustrations on you. Let them know it's okay to be angry. Sometimes what looks and feels like anger is really sorrow, and that's understandable.

Watch and wait for when your child is more willing to look on the bright side. When they are ready, help them research local attractions on the city's tourism website or anything that may appeal to your child's interests. Help make the move more tangible for them by showing them pictures of their future house, school, playground, or swimming pool. Children can begin to accept a move when they can visualize the next location, when it becomes more than a big question mark in their minds.

Reassure children they don't have to give up everything when they move. They can still keep in touch with their friends through email, text, video chat, and other ways. They can continue to play sports and be involved in school activities at the new location. Start looking for teams and clubs in the new place.

For a child who is particularly struggling with a move, enlist help from supportive teachers or coaches. These adults can help spot any changes in behavior that may indicate more serious issues. They can also help you communicate with your child and encourage them to talk about the new school and the new friends they will make. There are children's books about moving that will help your child know what to expect and how to voice their feelings.

It is also healthy for your child to have closure at the current location. Help them say goodbye to friends and favorite locations. Have a goodbye party or dinner and let them invite their friends. Ask them to journal or talk to you about their favorite memories from this duty station. Encourage them to make a scrapbook or a memory book for photos and messages from friends. Acknowledge the good times you have had here before turning the page to new opportunities. Acknowledge all they are sacrificing and give them closure to this stage of their life.

Your children may struggle to some degree every time you move, and it will be different for each child each time. Be patient and willing to listen to them. Reassure them their family is always there for them, no matter where you live. Use the resources provided by the military community, such as classes or counseling sessions, to help your child process this move.

Military life can be challenging, but it won't ruin your children's lives, far from it. Your kids can grow stronger and more resilient in these tough transition times, as long as you love and support them in healthy ways. Moving will be an adjustment for the whole family. You can't make it all easy and smooth for everyone. Your job as the parent is to be strong and supportive and lead your children through the roller coaster process. Even on the hard days, you can do that!

Open When
You Have a Long Drive Ahead

Dear Road Warrior,

Your next move is taking you to the other side of the country! And even though the military would reimburse plane tickets if you wanted to fly, you have decided it makes the most sense to drive your own vehicle. You'll avoid having to pay to ship a car or pets, and you can transport some of your own things yourselves. The military will pay a per diem related to your mileage to cover gas, food, and lodging. Maybe you're moving yourself and making some money at it. On paper at least, it makes sense to drive to the next duty assignment.

But now you've started thinking about spending several days with a car full of kids and pets and plants, and you're questioning your sanity before you even get started. Driving to a new duty station is among the rites of passage of military life, but if you're having second thoughts, you're certainly not the first person to wonder what this life has gotten you into. On top of the other stresses of a move, the logistics of planning for the long drive may seem like too much, let alone actually spending the hours and days behind the wheel.

On the other hand, you're also not the first person to pack up their belongings and travel across the country to start a new life. The pioneers come to mind. Their journey was filled with ridiculous obstacles. (I mean, have you ever tried to play the game Oregon Trail, only to have your entire party die of dysentery?) Luckily, in the modern age we have numerous tools and resources to help you move. You don't have to figure this all out on your own.

When planning your trip, start by choosing places to stop each night. If you just drive until you're tired each evening and start looking for a hotel, you may end up with poor accommodations and will probably pay higher hotel rates. Plan a full day of driving followed by a shorter day in the car. Look at maps to see what cities and interesting locations are in each area. Rooms with discounted rates are sometimes available on military installations, and you are not limited to your own service branch. However, you will need to call ahead to see if they have rooms available and make reservations. Be sure to mention the service member is traveling on military orders when you call. You will have precedence over those who are simply on vacation.

A long PCS drive becomes a lot more fun when you turn it into a road trip. Create your own silver lining and stop for a mini vacation to rest and relax for a day or two. Having a fun destination to break up the days of travel gives you something to look forward to. The military pays for a few days of travel, and if you're smart you can use that allowance to include a little sightseeing. You don't have to hit every National Park along the way—unless you want to—but if there is a place or two you'd like to visit, include it in your plan. It's an opportunity to see more of the country.

Consider staying with friends and family along the way too. Are there friends from former duty stations who live near your route? It's worth going a few miles out of your way to visit a friend or relative. Staying with friends or family is a great way to save money, but more importantly, it's a good way to reconnect and spend time with people you care about. They can encourage you during your journey.

You can also camp as you travel across the country. Camp sites are cheaper than hotel rooms and allow your family to visit some beautiful outdoor locations. This idea may work best if you are already a camping family and have the necessary gear and equipment. It takes a lot of planning to make sure you have enough food each day and the right clothing for various temperatures as you drive through different regions and climates. For your kids, camping will give them a chance to run around and explore after being in the car all day, which may help them settle down and sleep better than they would in a hotel room.

While we are on the subject of children, let's talk for a moment about the harsh reality of driving across the country with a car full of kids. If you're a parent, this is probably your biggest concern about the trip. You will need games and activities to keep them occupied in the car and snacks to quiet the munchies.

Children need more to occupy them than movies and video games, especially if the devices run out of battery charge. Find car-friendly ideas and create busy bags with games and activities they can pull out and play with on their own without unbuckling their seatbelts. Bring little toys or treats to hand out and celebrate every time you cross a new state line. Download kid-friendly audiobooks to play in the car for the whole family to enjoy. Go old-school and play travel games by searching for letters on signs or license plates. Sing songs. Kids won't remember the hours of wheat fields you drove past or the juice boxes they spilled on themselves. They will remember taking a trip and visiting new places together as you begin this new chapter.

Expect to make frequent rest stops and have an emergency back-up plan for accidents and car sickness. Keep a change of clothes for each child packed in an easy-to-reach location, along with wet wipes, towels, and plastic bags. Because with kids, it's almost guaranteed that messes and accidents will happen.

Any move is challenging, even if you stay in the same state. A big move involves more planning and research, but you will be thankful for your preparation. It's better to be overprepared and not need some of those contingency plans than to deal with a sudden emergency without a backup.

With a plan in place, there's no need to be fearful. These aren't the pioneer days of the Oregon Trail. You have phones and GPS, and one way or another, you will make it to your next duty station. You can probably avoid the dysentery too, and in the end, you will have some memorable—and possibly funny—stories to tell about your trip.

Something Precious Is Lost or Broken

Dear Relocated Loved One,

When everything you own is packed up and moved, there is always the chance something will be lost or broken. Accidents happen, mistakes are made. But knowing that doesn't make the heartache any easier when you get the gut-wrenching news some of your treasured possessions are gone forever.

You probably feel angry. When the military makes you move to a new location and then leaves you to suffer the consequences of careless government-hired movers, it feels like a double betrayal. If you moved yourselves, the anger is even closer to home. What was your spouse thinking when they put a heavy crate of tools on top of a box of fragile Christmas ornaments? Why weren't they more careful or thoughtful? Don't they know you can't just fly back to Europe and replace those precious things?

Yes, there may be the slight consolation of the reimbursement claims process. If the government moved you, they are responsible for paying for any lost or damaged items. There will be paperwork to fill out, a process to evaluate the value of your goods, and a wait to be reimbursed. If you moved yourselves, your own insurance may cover some of the damages. It may be worth filing a claim, even if the damaged items are mostly sentimental. In addition to the reimbursement, it can bring a sense of closure to the whole fiasco. Unfortunately, no amount of money can truly replace family heirlooms, broken souvenirs, or missing photo albums.

In those moments when you realize your precious belongings are truly gone, you must focus on one thing. Those objects were only important to you because of the people and memories they represent. People are always more important than stuff. Even if the people they remind you of are no longer with you, it's better to celebrate the memory of great people than to lament lost things. Those items cannot be replaced, but your fond memories are still with you. Focus on those positive memories and do what you can to honor them another way. Possibly you can download photos and create new scrapbooks or contact family members for copies of old photos. You can begin a new collection of Christmas ornaments and start new traditions with your family. If you have lost heirlooms from deceased relatives, make sure your children know the stories of those relatives. Write them down.

In the end, the stories, memories, and traditions are what you really wanted to preserve. Bring something positive out of your sad moving experience, so your family can move forward knowing what is truly lasting and worth holding onto. You didn't deserve this, but your love and your memories are strong enough to fill in the gaps for every precious item that was lost.

Open When
Starting Over Is Hard

Dear Uprooted Friend,

The trouble with moving every few years is that it's hard to feel at home. Sometimes it feels like you are temporarily camping out in a series of different houses. If you recently arrived at a new assignment and are having trouble adjusting, you probably feel like a stranger in a strange land. As hard as you try, you don't belong here. People are just different in this part of the country, and you wonder if you'll ever get used to it. Deep down, you wonder if it's worth the effort, since you probably won't live here very long anyway.

Loss of identity when you have to start all over again is one of the hardest parts of moving. Maybe you are between jobs or you've chosen to stay home with kids. Maybe losing a fulfilling social life has left an empty feeling. Moving is both physically and emotionally exhausting, and often a crash occurs soon after the essential boxes are unpacked. The process of starting over again and getting re-established in this new place feels daunting.

Hear me say this: what you feel is completely normal. For many military spouses it takes a few months or even a full year to start feeling comfortable and adjusted in a new place. If you aren't there yet, remember that getting settled doesn't happen automatically. It takes time and energy. For one thing, you are probably exhausted from the hard work of moving. You may not be ready to explore and get excited about your new town right now.

So instead of encouraging you to go full tourist, I say start with baby steps. The first thing to help you feel settled is finding your everyday essentials. Check out some grocery stores nearby. Attend worship or prayer services. Soon you will find your doctor, dentist, and hair salon, but you don't have to figure it all out today. Take it one place at a time. Go to the grocery store. Get milk, bread, and eggs … and ice cream.

Soon you will feel more comfortable here. You'll find your way to the gym without your GPS. You'll run into people you know at the library or at the park. Soon you'll be making plans to meet up with friends. Your everyday chores will become more natural, even routine. You will feel more at home here.

Feeling at home will take time—not only for you, but for the whole family. You will all need time to unpack the emotions and stress of the recent move, and each of you will have your own path to feeling more at home. You can help and support each other, but you can't rush the process. You have to go through the steps and stages to get there.

To help your family adjust, focus on some of the positive aspects of your new home. Sure, this town feels unfamiliar, and you aren't really sure what people do for fun around here. But there must be something you can do here that you couldn't do at the last place you lived! Brainstorm together to find ideas for local restaurants to try, places to visit, or daytrips to take. Try new local foods, different hiking trails, and local attractions to explore. If you don't know where to go first, check with Information, Tickets, and Travel at your installation and ask about military discount rates to local attractions and outings your family may enjoy. Planning activities as a family is a fun distraction from the newness of everything.

Physically making your new house a home is an important step toward adjusting. It may sound superficial but unpacking fully and decorating your home with familiar pictures and furniture will help the family feel more settled. It can be tempting to leave those boxes unpacked and not bother hanging anything on the walls, because you aren't going to be here that long, right? You could just camp out here with one foot out the door, biding your time until the military moves you again, but that's not a healthy way to view this move or the ones to come.

Think of each assignment in terms of time as well as place. If you will be there for a year or three years, ask yourself what you hope to do and accomplish in your time there. The time will be gone whether you use it well or not, so the best choice is to be intentional. Use it well.

Get comfortable within this place and time in your life. Hang the pictures. Paint the walls. Make the house your home. Buy the t-shirts for the new school or club. Even if you're only here for a short while, this is your home for now. The sooner you invest in it emotionally, the sooner it will begin to feel like home.

This stage is tough, my friend. It's hard when you are already physically and emotionally tired from moving, and you just feel alone and unsupported in your new place. Give it time. Take those baby steps. Look for the places and people that will make it feel more like home to you. Reach out and connect with one person or group, and then another. Soon you will make your first real friend. You'll discover a favorite restaurant. You will have a go-to place for family Saturdays or date nights.

You may not have it now, and that's okay. But believe me, it will happen for you in time. Keep putting yourself out there and making your best effort. You'll be surprised how much you come to love your new routines and your new life in your new home. Eventually, this place too will finally feel like a home where you belong.

Open When
You Need Friends in a New Place

Dear Friend Seeker,

Friends are an essential part of surviving military life. No matter how strong you are and how many times you have moved, you will always need a support system to lean on during difficult days and to celebrate with in good times. Now that the move is behind you, it's time to find those friends.

We all dream of having that one incredible friend, the one who totally gets us, puts up with our quirks and mood swings, and is always fun to be around. Maybe you already have a best friend, one who happens to live far from you right now. You don't have to replace your best friend each time you move. Long distance and lifelong friendships are necessary and sustaining. So are up close and everyday friendships. You may not find a new best friend at every location, but you will find good everyday friends if you reach out and look for them.

You do have to be purposeful and intentional about meeting and making nearby friends after a move. Friends on social media can offer words of support, but sometimes in military life you will need more than words. For example, who will you call if your car breaks down, or you need to go to the emergency room? Do you have a person to call? If not, then it's time to beef up your friend list.

I know, this is easier said than done. Sometimes a friendship will show up on your doorstep in the form of a friendly neighbor, but you can't always wait for friends to come to you. Be intentional and seek them out. Surrounding yourself with positive people and good influences will make you a stronger person.

When you are out and about, whether waiting in line at the commissary or picking up kids at school, be brave. Take the first step and strike up a conversation. Think of it like speed dating, but for new friendships.

Join a gathering with your family readiness group, spouse club, chapel, or bowling league. If the event is a yawner for you, look for someone else stifling a yawn. There, now you have something in common! Look for other places to connect, such as gym classes, play groups, local sports leagues, faith communities, or any group activity that appeals to you.

Keep connecting and building up your contact list of friends. Don't stop with one friend, and don't expect one person to meet all your friendship needs. Here are a few of the different kinds of friends who can make your military life easier and more enjoyable:

The Emergency Contact: The first neighbor you meet will probably be listed on all your children's emergency paperwork for a while, just because they are the only person whose phone number you know in this time zone. Don't be afraid to update this as you meet and get to know more people.

The Battle Buddy: You may resist the idea of connecting to other military spouses or significant others, but trust me, their support can be invaluable. Ideally, this is someone whose loved one is in the same unit as yours who will be there for you during deployments. This friend could become the person you will text late at night because you know they're awake; the one who will cry with you over communication blackouts and rejoice with you about homecoming. No one quite understands deployment like another military spouse, which is why you should be friends with at least one other military spouse or loved one. My guess is you won't be able to stop with just one.

The Workout Partner: If you're trying to stay healthy, you will be more successful with this partner at your side. Maybe you walk the dogs together, take a class at the gym, or sign up for a 5K race together. Encourage each other to reach your personal best!

The Handy One: It's not a question of if things will go wrong, but when. And the answer is usually when your service member is away. Luckily, this handy friend or their spouse has a complete tool set and knows a thing or two about cars, appliances, or maintenance items you are less familiar with or that require more than one person to manage. Keep them on speed dial.

The Adventurer: This is the friend who is always up for trying something new and getting out of the house. Make a bucket list of day trips or quirky local places to visit and do it together.

The Local Expert: This friend grew up near the base and can tell you all about what to eat, and where to find a good dentist, salon, or mechanic. They also love to hear your stories about other parts of the country and the world.

The Prayer Partner: Finding a new church or faith community you love can make a new duty station feel like home. This buddy will invite you into the community, make you feel welcome at meetings, and pray with you and for you when life is rough.

Making friends is an incredibly important part of settling in at a new place. For the unique situations of military life, it's helpful to have friends who understand because they live this life too. They can offer support and sympathy when you are dealing with frequent trainings, deployment, waiting on orders, and other challenges of military life. It's nice to have someone who doesn't require an explanation of these demands. Many other military spouses are also looking for friendship, and deep down, we aren't strangers. We are all part of this military community, and we can all use the extra support.

Don't overlook the importance of having friends in the civilian world too. Obviously, friends of all kinds enrich our lives in many ways and help us connect to the community and all it has to offer.

You may not know them yet, but plenty of wonderful people both in and out of the military community want to be your friend. It's up to you to find them and connect with them. The more people you meet, the more friends you will make, and the stronger your support network will be. You will have help when you need it and you'll be able to help others when they need it. Remember, we are all stronger when we are together!

Open When
Your Child Struggles at a New School

Dear Loving Parent,

When your child has to change schools because of a move, it can be hard on both of you. Whether or not they were happy at their last school, it may take some time for them to feel comfortable at their new one. They might blame you, and you might end up blaming yourself. After all, it isn't your child's fault they are starting over at a new school.

There are no quick fixes for the adjustment period after a move. The only way forward is to make the most of it. Focus on ways to help your child make this transition.

Change can be challenging—for everyone. Let your child voice their complaints; listen to their concerns. Help them see all the benefits of the new school, but let them know they can tell you when they're having a hard time. Give them a safe place to express their emotions, whether positive or negative. Be their trusted partner to help them through the adjustment process. Hug them when they cry. Be a listening ear when they need to vent and allow them to miss their old school. But then offer positive solutions for moving forward and carving out a niche for themselves in the new place.

Encourage a sense of adventure. Help your child check out local sports teams, clubs, hobbies, scout groups, or other interests, so they can find a group of friends and experience a sense of belonging.

Before your student's first day at a new school, take time to visit the school and do a walk-through. Set up meetings with teachers, and if possible, look for ways to meet future classmates too. Anything you can do to add some familiarity will help them on their first day.

Ask at the new school about resources for military families. They may have a military kids club, or maybe you can start one. Some schools have groups for kids going through deployment or have a military family night once a month. Some have free after-school tutoring programs for military kids. Your installation's school liaison officer (SLO) may also be able to help.

For concerns about your child's customized learning plan or academic credits being transferred to a new school, read up on the provisions of the Interstate Compact on Educational Opportunity for Military Children, which covers these and other transition issues.

At school or at home, every time your child takes a step toward being more comfortable in their new place, celebrate with them. Give them encouragement and incentives to keep trying. Show them that you see they are doing their best.

It's normal for military kids to struggle for a bit when adjusting to a new school. Moving is emotional and exhausting, and kids need time to process everything happening to them. They may act out in the classroom or at home. They may also refuse to respect a new teacher or neglect their homework. Enlist support from educators to help you and your child through these struggles. Communicate regularly with teachers and school counselors. It can sometimes take a while for grades to bounce back after a move. Remind your child you love them and are proud of them, regardless of the grade on the report card.

Staying in close communication with educators can also help you and your child determine if an issue they are facing is caused by something other than their latest move.

Finally, don't get caught up in guilt. Your children will face many experiences beyond their control. You can teach them this fact of life while they are still safe in your care. Adjusting to change is a valuable skill, and children adjust best when they know they are loved and supported. Keep giving hugs and hope. Your child may be struggling now, but they will get through this, and you have the power to help them. Be a strong role model for them and show them how to handle difficult life challenges. These are skills your child will have forever and possibly thank you for one day. So hang in there! This is a difficult stage to get through, but it is one you and your child can face together.

Open When
You're Stuck in Temporary Housing With Kids

Dear Frazzled Parent,

As if moving wasn't hard enough, now you are trapped in this transitional no man's land, perhaps living in limited space out of suitcases. It's common for military families to spend some time in a hotel, temporary housing, or simply an empty house while waiting for their household goods to arrive. Or you could be on the waiting list for military housing. This is especially true if you move overseas or return from overseas, when it takes months for your furniture to travel over the ocean. All these circumstances are common, but that doesn't make them any easier.

So here you are, stuck in a small space with your children, trying to figure out what to do with them and how to allow everyone a decent amount of sleep each night. Meanwhile, your service member has their own concerns. Maybe they've returned to work and are spending a good part of each day on duty, even if they're still in-processing. If you're a one-car family—even if only temporarily—you may not have a lot of options for entertaining the kids. You wish you could get a few moments of peace and quiet, or just a tiny bit of personal space. You would even settle for a good night's sleep without someone in the family waking up everyone else at the crack of dawn!

If you are reading this before your move and you already know you'll be in cramped quarters for a while, you can prepare. You may only spend a few days in a hotel, which anyone can deal with. But if it stretches into a week or longer, you'll need a way to save your sanity.

If you are moving overseas or returning from an overseas assignment, the way you plan your express shipment—the one that should arrive at your new location around the same time you do—

makes all the difference. Use this small shipment wisely, considering that your space might be limited. Include enough clothes to keep you from having to do laundry every day. Pack favorite blankets and stuffed animals to help children sleep well.

Take along collapsible strollers or a wagon, so you'll have a way to get out and about with kids in tow. If you know you will have enough space, you could also include bicycles in your express shipment. And include rainy-day activities: books, toys, movies, art supplies, and games. You could also purchase a few new items either before you leave—and add them to the express shipment—or after you arrive. Having something new to play with, discover, or learn can brighten up the long days.

If you are doing a move within the United States, you won't have an express shipment, but you can use the same strategy when deciding what to pack in your car or suitcases to have with you during the trip and before your household goods arrive. Setting these items aside before the move will make your transition time a little more bearable.

Perhaps you're already stuck in hotel limbo, and you don't have much to work with. All is not lost. First, keep the children's schedule as close as possible to what they were used to before the move. If they're young and used to afternoon naps, get them out and about in the morning for a change of scenery and to tire them out for naptime. Find a park or playground where you can play together, read books, or have a picnic in the fresh air. Take a nature walk to explore and check out flowers, leaves, and rocks. Turn it into a game by creating nature Bingo or a scavenger hunt. Getting out and about will relieve the cabin fever and help you all get to know the neighborhood or area.

If you have bikes or a car to help you get around town, then use this time to explore. Find the nearest library and get a library card for access to new books and movies. If the library offers regular story and craft times, or after school programs, you've hit the jackpot.

If you have a vehicle, get out and explore your new hometown. If you're in military temporary housing, chances are you have a swimming pool, gym, movie theater, or bowling alley nearby. Most have free or discounted access to anyone with a military ID card. The novelty of exploring new locations will help wear out the kids without making you wear out yourself or your wallet.

At bedtime, it's certainly difficult to get all the children to sleep when you're sharing a room, and then there is no way for you and your spouse to share any quiet time together. If you keep them active during the day, spend time in the sunlight, and avoid too much screen time, they will settle more naturally into their bedtime routine.

Take a family walk in the evening to let the kids work off their excess wiggles before bath time. Stick with traditional winding down routines, such as stories or music. If you and your spouse need space to talk, find a place to sit outside the hotel room or house. You can still keep an eye on your little ones, but your conversations won't keep them awake. This may be a good opportunity for the adults to practice going to bed earlier too. You and your spouse both need the extra sleep to recover from the stress of moving. You'll also appreciate the extra energy in the mornings, since your family is probably waking up earlier than usual.

Taking care of kids in cramped quarters is not ideal. You are probably longing for extra space, your own furniture, and all the comforts of home. It seems like a long wait, but you will eventually have it all again. Living out of suitcases won't last forever, even though sometimes it feels like it.

Try to find a few moments each day to step back and enjoy being with your kids and have fun with them. When you are all back to your regular busy routines, you won't always have such concentrated family time. Even though it's difficult, savor the small gifts of this in-between time. Your household goods and your housing assignment will arrive soon, just in time to save the last shreds of your sanity.

Open When

You're Adjusting to Life in Another Country

Dear Expatriate,

Maybe you never wanted to live in another country, or maybe this is the overseas assignment you always wanted. Either way, here you are, and it's much harder than you thought it would be. Yes, you expected life in another country to be different. You expected the language barrier to be a challenge, but you didn't expect everything to be a barrier. Every single task is different and more difficult than it needs to be, from parking the car to doing laundry to stopping by the grocery store. You don't know anyone. You don't know the streets or how to read the confusing road signs. And you miss the convenience and familiarity of home way more than you thought you would.

There is no one to talk to who understands your isolation. Your family is all on the other side of the world, thousands of miles and several time zones away. You feel disconnected from them. Your friends back in the US are all envious of your assignment and seem to think you are on some kind of exotic vacation with no reason to complain. And the people you've met at your new location just shrug when they hear your struggles and say, "You'll get used to it," or "That's how it is here." You don't feel at home yet, and you certainly don't feel like you're on vacation. Some days you are simply exhausted and defeated. You wish you could throw your hands up in the air and go back to home, but that's not an option.

Moving to another country is a huge adjustment, and it will take time before you feel comfortable and begin to enjoy the experience. The first few weeks, especially, are completely overwhelming, so don't push yourself too hard. Set reasonable expectations and goals. You'll be taking baby steps for a while, and that's okay. When every task is frustrating, you have to celebrate each tiny win.

One of my friends says the adjustment to life in another country is like building a charm bracelet. When you first arrive, your bracelet is just a blank, empty chain. You need to treasure every small success like a new charm. When you venture to a grocery store off base, that's a charm to add to your bracelet. You figured out parking in the narrow downtown streets? Another charm. When you order a local dish at a restaurant, explore the market, or learn a new word, those are more charms dangling from your wrist. In time, your bracelet will be crowded and full of experiences. There will be times you can add those precious gems like weekend travel, getting approved for a job on base, or having a conversation with a new non-American friend. But you have to build it all one single charm at a time.

For now, everything is new. Challenge yourself to take one small new step each day, and one bigger step each week. In the beginning, everything is hard, but you can do hard things, even scary things. One step at a time, you will learn your way around, and soon nothing will seem so hard or scary anymore.

To get a toehold in this foreign land, find someone else who is already settled and has lived here for a while and ask them about the basics: grocery shopping, stores, restaurants, and setting up phones. Slowly but surely, you will figure out a new way of life here. The language and customs may still seem foreign, but your lifestyle will be predictable and manageable.

When you feel homesick for your family and for your home country, think of a few special foods or items to remind you of home and order them if you can't find them at the commissary or local stores. Or you can ask family and friends to send you a care package. These can be a refreshing treat when you are feeling far from home. Just don't count on two-day delivery.

An even better way to combat homesickness is to get out and explore. Even though everything feels strange and difficult, exploring your local town will help you appreciate your new assignment. Try something simple like going for a short walk in the downtown neighborhood or taking a day trip in the area. Ask another family to show you their favorite restaurant. As you discover the unique features of your new place, you will slowly begin to appreciate and feel comfortable in your new home.

If it doesn't feel like home yet, just wait. You'll get there. One day, you won't be the new family anymore. It won't happen tomorrow, but it will sneak up on you and suddenly you'll realize you're there. You'll be the one giving out directions and helping others. You will be zipping around the downtown streets and maybe even parallel parking like a champ. You will have a favorite restaurant and a weekend destination, and you'll be recommending them to the new arrivals. By then, your charm bracelet of experiences will be filled with beautiful memories and fun stories.

For now, take one day at a time, one task at a time. You will grow in confidence every day. Your new home has so much to offer you. It will take time to appreciate it, but you have time on your side. Everyone you know who seems settled and comfortable overseas started out right where you are now. Give yourself time and keep trying. Keep doing the hard things, and soon you'll be doing seemingly impossible things you never imagined. And you'll be home.

Open When
You're Grieving Your Previous Duty Station

Dear Homesick Loved One,

Sometimes, a place works its way into your heart until it feels like home and you never want to leave. Your experiences from all the places you live will be with you forever. Each location becomes a part of who you are, but some places will be harder to leave than others. In time, you learn to love both your old home and your new one, treasuring the memories from both.

Sometimes your heart takes longer than your household goods to move on from one duty station to the next. When you leave a place you love, the new place seems to have nothing to offer. Even when you know you should get out and explore the new location, all you can think about is your old home. It was beautiful there. You were comfortable there. You had friends there. In comparison, this new location has no appeal yet. You keep feeling a mixture of frustration and great sadness every time you look at photos or see social media posts about your previous assignment.

If this is happening to you, it may be difficult to describe your emotions. While you know rationally you can't go back and you need to settle in, your heart refuses to call this new place home. "Home" is the duty station you just left, the one you loved, where you have so many friends and memories. You may wonder how you can be homesick for a place where you only lived temporarily, but you can. Perhaps you are experiencing emotional swings, and you don't know what to do about them. It may surprise you to learn what you are going through is grief.

At first, it sounds like an exaggeration to use the term grief to describe homesickness. If you have lost family members before, you know the depth of emotions at the loss of a person does not compare to the sadness of moving. But any loss results in some form of grief, and when you leave a place you love it is a loss. Military families lose a lot when they move. You have every right to grieve. Having a word for what you are feeling will help you make sense of it.

The more you know about the grief process, the easier it will be to identify what you are going through when you move. There are stages of grief, and military families report going through some or all of them after a difficult move. You may not go through the stages in order, as if you were accomplishing a five-step checklist. Instead, you may spend several weeks in one stage, or you might swing through three different stages in one day. You might move back and forth through different stages, repeating one, getting stuck in another for a while, or skipping some altogether.

First, you may be in denial. When you receive orders to the new location, it doesn't feel real. You may go through the motions of researching the next base, but part of you is holding your breath to see if the orders will change. Even after you move, you are resisting calling this new place your home.

When in the grip of denial, surround yourself with specifics. The more details you can get about your new location, the more real it will seem. Before you get there, if you know where you are living, ask someone to take a picture of the house or of comparable military or civilian housing. Look at a map of your new area. Learn how it looks and get familiar with street names. When you arrive, find popular local restaurants and try the specialties. Go for walks to appreciate the views. You will still miss your old home, but you will have tangible connections to your new home too.

At some point, you may feel anger. Your anger might be directed toward your new duty station: *Why are the stupid streets so confusing here?* or your spouse: *Why did you make us move here?* or the military: *Don't they know how hard this is for our kids?* There are healthy ways to express anger once you recognize why you are angry. When you realize you are angry because you have no new friends, or because your career progression was interrupted, or because the children are having trouble adjusting, your emotions will make more sense and become more manageable. Write about what makes you angry in a journal, or talk it out with your spouse, a parent, or trusted friend. You can also channel it into a hobby like music, exercise, or cooking. Be honest with yourself and your spouse about the anger you feel. Find ways to channel it and vent it, but don't feed it, and it won't last forever.

You may have reached the bargaining stage if you say things like, *If we move there, at least I will save money/get a job/go back to school/ lose weight.* This can be a way of looking for positives in a new place. However, if your satisfaction is based on those expectations and they aren't fulfilled quickly after the move, you could be setting yourself up for disappointment. Be conscious of your expectations and keep them realistic. Don't make promises to yourself or your children you may not be able to keep. If you are a list person, make a pro and con list of the duty station you're leaving that you loved so much. Being clear-sighted about the good and bad at the old location may help you realize there's good and bad in your new assignment, too.

Any time you experience major life changes and losses, it is possible to experience some level of depression. You may feel sad, lethargic, and uninterested in activities. Talk to your spouse about your feelings. Your actions can help reduce some of these effects. Be sure you get out in the fresh air and sunshine. Make plans you can look forward to—a visit to a new restaurant, a walk in the park, or coffee with a new friend or neighbor. Keep an eye on your symptoms and triggers. If feelings of sadness hang on longer than you think they should, if they interfere with your sleep cycle or ability to get through your daily activities, or if you are simply not sure about your symptoms, don't hesitate to consult with your doctor or mental health professional.

For any move, acceptance is the goal—becoming comfortable and adjusted in your new home. It may take you just a few weeks, or it can take a year or more to feel at home in a new duty station. It's okay if this process takes a long time instead of happening all at once. Acceptance of a new home can happen in little pieces, and sometimes it may feel like taking one step forward and two steps back. You may make a new friend one day, but it could take weeks before you remember the route to the local store without GPS. It's normal to accept some circumstance, but still be in another stage of grief about others. It may take a long time to adjust. Celebrate each small accomplishment. Treasure those moments, and on bad days recall the sense of accomplishment and victory. You've earned it!

Moving can be hard, my friend, and grieving your last home is sometimes part of the process. When you move, you have to unpack more than just cardboard boxes. You need to take the time to unpack your emotions and process the major changes you have just gone through. If you're feeling grieved, take the time to admit your feelings and work through them. You are not alone.

Sealed With a Kiss

My Story
Alone in the Storm

I sat in the darkened hallway of the hospital, clutching my newborn son while a storm raged outside. Several other mothers like me had babies who arrived alongside a hurricane in Camp Lejeune, on the coast of North Carolina. Unlike me, however, the other new mothers were accompanied by a spouse or a parent. My husband, Dan, was in Afghanistan, and my mom was at home with my other two children. I was alone in the storm.

We knew from the beginning Dan would not be home for the birth of this baby. We knew he would deploy when I was eight months pregnant. Still, it took me half the pregnancy to come to terms with that fact. No woman wants to give birth alone.

Making plans helped me cope and feel more in control of the situation. I asked my mom to come to stay for a few weeks at our home to help care for our other two children, a three-year-old and eighteen-month-old. I invited a close friend and mom of four to be on call to go with me to the hospital and hold my hand. I also found a doula, or birth coach, who offered free service to expectant moms with deployed husbands. Having arranged for a birth coach, a friend, and childcare at home, I had done my best to prepare for what I knew was coming.

Then came news of the hurricane. As my due date neared, the storm approached the East Coast. In preparation, the base was shutting down, and many people were evacuating—including the friend who had planned to be at the hospital with me. Forty weeks into my pregnancy, I wasn't able to travel even a few hours inland. I couldn't evacuate. My mom and I prepared to ride out the coming storm, stocking up on bottled water and canned food, even tarps in case of storm damage to our home. I stayed busy, going through the motions of storm preparations. Inside, I just felt helpless and overwhelmed. I walked and walked around our neighborhood in the sticky North

Carolina heat, trying to convince the baby to arrive ahead of the storm. He took his time.

Finally, the day before the storm made landfall, I went into labor. I spent most of the day at home trying to relax and time my contractions. In the middle of the Afghanistan desert, Dan didn't have a phone or computer, but he was able to check on me daily via satellite phone after I passed my due date. When I went into labor, he got permission to spend the day in the unit communications tent, so he could stay in touch with me throughout the day. We didn't have video or audio connection, but we were able to communicate by typing messages to each other via Google Hangouts. Being connected to my husband, even in such a simple way, helped me feel stronger and calmer about delivering alone.

By evening, my contractions were steady, and I was ready to go to the hospital. The doula drove me to the hospital while my mom stayed at home with my other kids. The doula helped me get checked in and settled into a birthing room but then told me one of her paying clients had also gone into labor that night. (The pressure drop during a hurricane causes a lot of women to go into labor.) Because I was a pro bono client, she called another doula to come stay with me, so she could attend to her other client. That left me in the labor room with someone I had never met before. Of course, I would rather have had Dan with me, but the doula helped me with my breathing, medical choices, and made me as comfortable as possible throughout the birthing process.

Near midnight, as winds whipped the pine trees around the hospital, I typed a message to Dan:

Getting ready to push!

A few minutes later, we sent him an image of his newborn son. The baby was healthy, and I was exhausted. But I felt a tremendous sense of pride. I had conquered the obstacle I had been dreading for nine months, giving birth by myself.

The brunt of the hurricane hit about the time I was moved into a recovery room. Fallen trees had taken down power lines throughout the area, and power was out at the hospital. Emergency generators supplied power to the birthing floor, but not on the recovery floor where I was trying to sleep after giving birth. A nurse brought me a flashlight, so I could find my way to the bathroom. An hour later, she came in again to tell me we were under tornado watch. All patients were being moved away from the windows into the hallway. By then it was 4 a.m. I carried my newborn baby into the hallway, joining the other moms, dads, and newborns huddled together.

And that's how I ended up sitting alone in a dark hallway, cradling my baby and praying the tornadoes wouldn't hit the house where my other children and my mom were sleeping. Our family was stretched too far apart, I thought as I sat there, trying to hold back my tears. I had made it through childbirth with determination, medication, and a stranger holding my hand, but as the weather threatened outside, I felt terrified and vulnerable.

When the storm warning passed, I was able to go back to my room and sleep after being awake for twenty-four hours. The next day, even though my doctor was ready to discharge me, I couldn't leave. The base was still shut down, and roads were closed due to fallen trees. Instead of going home, I moved down to another floor where the doctors' families were sheltering during the storm. Without power, the hospital was not able to provide hot meals. I had to walk down several flights of stairs, carrying the baby, to get a meal from a food truck. That was my first meal after giving birth. When the roads re-opened on the third day, my mom was finally able to pick me up, and it was such a relief to get back home where I could rest and eat!

While my story is dramatic, I want you to know that there's nothing special or magical about me that enabled me to get through this ordeal. You have the same strength and ability to conquer difficult situations. Military families have been navigating these challenges for hundreds of years.

Sometimes deployment feels lonely, dark, and dangerous, as it did when I huddled in the dark hospital hallway alone with my new baby. Then and many other times during Dan's seven deployments, I have been fearful and discouraged. The deployment when our son was born was one of our most challenging chapters. I have been in the dark hallway of deployment many times, and I'm here on the other side to let you know you can get through those difficult times.

Deployment has a way of throwing unexpected roadblocks in your way. Do what you can to prepare for challenges, the way I prepared by having a doula, the way my mom and I stocked up on food and water for the hurricane. However, all the planning in the world can't prevent the unexpected, so remain flexible and ready to meet changing circumstances. I couldn't have anticipated my friend wouldn't be able to be with me, or the power outage at the hospital. I had to face these situations as they happened.

I've dealt with my fair share of frustrations during deployment, from broken appliances to car trouble to sick kids. There have been plenty of times when I was exhausted and wanted to throw in the towel. Possibly because of everything that could and did go wrong, I have also witnessed incredible kindness. I'm thankful I discovered resources and learned to lean on my support system. It certainly hasn't been easy, but one way or another, each deployment has made me stronger than I was before.

Open When

You First Learn About Deployment Orders

Dear Bewildered Friend,

So you just got the news your spouse is going to deploy. Maybe the deployment is months or even a year from now, or maybe your service member will leave in just a few weeks or days. Either way, deployment news can ruin your plans for the coming months and change the trajectory of your life.

If you're crying, that's okay. If you're angry at the military or even at your spouse, that's normal too. We've all felt that way before about deployment orders. Military life doesn't always happen the way you expect. Maybe you were promised a non-deployable assignment for a few years, and everything just changed. Maybe you've been trying to have a baby, and this delays your hopes for another year. It's natural to feel upset, scared, and overwhelmed. Don't be afraid of your emotions; they reflect what is happening to you. Deployment is a big deal, and it affects everything in your life.

Ignore those who say, "You knew what you were getting into," or "This is what you signed up for," when you fell in love with a service member. Even people who go into military life with their eyes wide open don't always know how to handle the flood of emotion that comes with deployment orders. Even those who have been through deployment before have feelings about each new set of orders. Just because you love your service member doesn't mean you have to love this part of your relationship.

The important question is: *How will you get through this?*

Right now, maybe you aren't sure, and you feel like you just can't do it. It's too much, too long, too difficult. But you are stronger than you think. Sooner or later, every military loved one faces a situation they thought they couldn't handle, yet they do. They discover a measure of hidden inner strength they didn't know they had. And you will too.

You will get through this, just as millions of military loved ones have gone through deployments and combat tours and wars before you. Many like you are going through it right now. You aren't alone in your struggle.

One step at a time, one day at a time, you and your service member will conquer deployment. It will not be easy. There will almost certainly be bad days. But you know what? It won't be bad every single day, even while you are apart. There will be good days too.

Deployment is a season. It may feel like a strange and unnatural season, but it's not forever. It won't always be like this. Do what you need to do to get yourself ready for the deployment and feel prepared to face it. On the days when you just feel face-down in the muck with no hope, don't forget to look up and find something to look forward to.

Many people handle the stress and uncertainty of deployment by trying to get organized and make plans. You can't control the deployment, and I know that is extremely frustrating. But there's plenty you can control. You get to decide where and how you will spend this time. You can control who you become friends with and what hobbies you pursue. You can choose to set goals, save money, work out, re-organize the house, and eat healthier. If you focus on those choices, on what is still up to you, you will be more confident about the deployment.

Right now, the deployment stretching out in front of you seems impossibly long. But time will keep marching on, and there will come a day when this deployment is behind you. When that day comes, how will you wish you had spent your time? Spend it that way, and you will have fewer regrets. Start now to think about your goals and dreams. Have you always wanted to go back to school, travel, or learn a new skill? Deployment may be the perfect opportunity. Despite the general negatives of military deployments, there are usually a few silver linings too. Focusing on positive goals and milestones will keep you going through the rough days.

Deployment is difficult, but you can get through it. There will be plenty of days with tears and heartache, but you will also discover inner reserves of strength and courage you didn't know you had. Today you may be feeling an emotional mess, and that's okay. Tomorrow you are going to get up and face this deployment. You will begin to plan and prepare. Treasure the remaining family time and holidays before departure. Gear up by building your tribe and gathering resources.

You will find strength to anchor you during the challenging times of deployment. So hang on for tomorrow, because it will get better.

Open When

You Want to Feel Prepared

Dear Hopeful Organizer,

When you are facing deployment, it feels like a big unknown, but there are some practical ways you can prepare. Every military spouse learns from experience to expect the unexpected, especially during deployment. Of course, you can't predict the future, but you can prepare for some of the possibilities. Instead of worrying about those situations ahead of time, you can use this time before deployment to plan and prepare.

Planning and practical action help reduce some of the uncertainty you are feeling about deployment. You'll have more peace of mind knowing you are as prepared as possible.

It helps to create a deployment binder to organize all your preparations and lists and to keep all your essential paperwork in one place. When the need arises, you will know exactly where to go to find the information or support you need. You can put any important information in your binder. A few essentials are:

- Copy of your spouse's deployment orders
- Power of attorney to allow you to act on your spouse's behalf when necessary
- Family care plan to prepare for any emergencies
- Password list so you have access to all your accounts and bills
- Personal contact list
- Instructions for sending a Red Cross message
- Directory of your installation

It's a good idea to update your ID card before a deployment, because getting it renewed is more complicated when your service member isn't with you. Along with your ID, there are other important documents to update before departure, including your wills and your service member's emergency contact form. This form names the individuals to be informed in case of an emergency, so be sure you are listed with correct marital status and contact information.

Review your budget and bills. Household income and expenses can change during deployment, especially if the spouse at home has to cut back work hours or pay for additional expenses like childcare or lawn maintenance. Your service member may receive additional income during deployment as well. Either way, discuss the changes and decide together how your budget will shift during deployment.

Decide who will pay bills and when they need to be paid. Be sure that person has all the necessary passwords and information. Set up automatic payments or allotments to take some tasks off your list. Be sure to keep track of and account for any automatic transactions. Alert your bank or credit card company your service member will be traveling or out of the country.

After your finances and paperwork are in order, give your house a check-up. Walk through your house together and make sure the spouse remaining behind knows the location of circuit breakers and the main water shut off. Review upcoming maintenance on any major appliances or systems and have routine maintenance done or scheduled if possible.

Have your vehicles checked out and make sure regular maintenance is done. You could save yourself a lot of trouble by replacing worn tires or changing the oil now, rather than waiting for a flat or a breakdown. If you don't plan to use a second vehicle during deployment, discuss storage and maintenance options.

Most importantly, what do you need to keep yourself in good running order? Think ahead for any routine doctor and dentist appointments you can schedule before deployment.

Finally, in the days leading up to deployment, don't forget to spend time and have fun together. As you can see, it's easy to get caught up in the long list of necessary tasks. Making time for each other is also important, whether you can get away for a weekend or just for a few hours. Take some photos of your time together.

The more you plan and prepare, the better you will be able to handle both routine and emergency situations during deployment. It takes some effort now to avoid major headaches later.

If your loved one receives deployment orders on short notice, you may not have time to do everything on this list. Don't panic! Focus first on the tasks only your service member can do in person, starting with powers of attorney and updating wills, if needed. Get copies of deployment orders, account passwords, and emergency contacts for your service member's family. Also plan a date night or time together. You can't do that without your loved one.

Military life sometimes requires you to move forward without as much planning or preparation as you might like, but you will make it through. Don't hesitate to ask for help and support or accept it when it is offered. You will find many helping hands and willing friends.

Open When
It's Time to Tell Your Children

Dear Concerned Parent,

It was bad enough when you first heard the deployment news yourself. You've cried, and complained, and gone through waves of anger and frustration. But now you have to deal with the next enormous challenge—telling the kids. Just thinking about it probably breaks your heart and brings you close to tears again.

You will feel a mixture of guilt and dread when it's time to break the news about deployment to your kids. You want to protect your children from emotional pain whenever you can, but it's almost impossible to shield military kids from the pain of being apart from their service-member parent. Your feelings and concerns about their reactions can make this a difficult conversation to have. However, it's something you must do intentionally and in a timely way, so they don't accidentally learn about deployment by overhearing your adult conversations.

How and when to tell your kids will depend mostly on their ages. Very young children, up to about age five, don't have a good sense of the passage of time. Young children may also have difficulty understanding complex situations and expressing their emotions. It may be confusing and upsetting for them to know about a deployment several months ahead, so it might be better to wait and tell them a few weeks out. The exact timing is, of course, according to your judgment about your child's needs and ability to understand.

If at all possible, tell your child about the deployment when the service member parent is present to share the news, so they can reassure the child of their love.

Use the word "deployment" and the name of the country, even if the child has never heard of it before. Don't simply say their military parent is "going to work" for a long time. Younger children may associate that with their parent's work location on base or post. They will be confused about why Mom or Dad can't come home every night or for special occasions if they are simply "at work."

Keep in mind you and your service member are probably telegraphing your emotions about the deployment without meaning to, even before you tell your children. If they are perceptive, no matter what their age, they may already know something is up—or they may overhear adult conversations. If they begin to ask questions, give them honest answers on a level they can understand.

Older children may need time to process the deployment, prepare themselves emotionally, and store up good experiences with their deploying parent. They may want to spend extra time together bonding before deployment. School-age children will want to know whether or not the deployment will affect their school year, sports activities, or birthday plans. For these reasons, you may want to tell older children about deployment several months in advance. This gives you time to celebrate missed birthdays and holidays before departure.

When telling older children or teens the news of deployment, be prepared for a range of emotions: silence, a lot of questions, indifference, or a negative emotional reaction. Your child may demonstrate all of the above at various times, possibly all on the same day. It's a lot to take in—and not just for them. Take their reactions in stride without passing judgment on their feelings. Let them express how they feel. Answer questions as much as you can and let them know you are there for them when they want to talk. Don't push if they're not ready. Later, be sensitive to opportunities when your child might be ready to talk. Make it easy for them to bring up the subject, or, if your child responds well to direct questions, just ask if they have questions or want to talk. Let them take the lead and let them know you are there for them whenever they are ready.

Even if your child has been through deployment before, don't assume it will be any easier for them to accept. Remember how much they have grown and changed since then. Treat each deployment as a first, because it is the first for a child at the age they are now. Be prepared for different questions, emotions, and reactions than they may have had before.

While it is understandable that both you and your child will struggle with difficult emotions, it is up to you to lead them by example. Demonstrate ways to be strong and encouraging when facing adversity. For a positive focus, discuss ways you will celebrate together before, during, or after the deployment. Talk about specific ways they can communicate with their parent during deployment. This can include email, care packages, photo apps, and video calls. Sometimes when service members have internet available, they are able to play online games with the family. Download some to try out before the deployment begins. Kids will realize they are not powerless in the face of deployment when they know they can take action and find ways to stay in contact with their beloved parent.

It's common for children to feel anger—at the military for taking their parent away or even at the parent who is leaving. Let them voice their emotions and talk about their feelings. Empathize with them and emphasize you will all work together to help and support each other through the deployment.

Children often benefit from having tangible ways to visualize deployment. If it helps your children, you can create a display in your home about the deployment. Make it as simple or as elaborate as you like and include the elements your children understand: photos or drawings of your service member, a calendar countdown of deployment days, a map and time zone clock for the deployment location. You may choose to add a calendar when you are near the end of deployment, if the pages or months from beginning to end seem overwhelming.

Children of any age may have concerns about their parent's safety during deployment. Answer questions about the service member's duties according to the child's age and ability to understand. Reassure them their parent is well trained and will be protected by military equipment and security measures, along with their fellow service members.

If you need additional support when talking to your kids about deployment, there are programs available to your military family. For kids in school, check with a school counselor or school liaison officer (SLO) for details about local resources for kids with deployed parents.

For children of any age, information about confidential counseling resources is available at the family center or through your family's primary care provider.

It's never easy to tell your kids about an upcoming deployment. Seeing their raw emotion makes it so much more real and painful for you too. It is always best to be honest and open with them, encouraging them to be honest with you about their deployment emotions. Focus on your remaining time as a family and making fun memories together as you prepare for the journey ahead.

Open When
You Will Give Birth
Without Your Spouse

Dear Parent-To-Be,

So you recently learned you're pregnant, and your baby will be born while your spouse is deployed. Whether this pregnancy is a surprise or has been planned for a long time, it's still a shock to realize you may have to bring your baby into the world without your service member by your side. You are probably experiencing a whirlwind of emotions, happy and sad, thankful and fearful, elated or even angry.

This mixture of positive and negative feelings is a completely normal reaction to a very daunting situation. And let's be honest—those pregnancy hormones do a number on your emotions, even in the calmest of situations.

On the other hand, you may be feeling a bit numb. If you will go through pregnancy and birth during the deployment, it may take a long time before you feel excited or accepting of the pregnancy. It might even bother you to have people congratulate you and your spouse. You might paste on a smile and say, "thank you," while on the inside you are frustrated and overwhelmed. It's okay. You have nine months to prepare. You don't have to figure it all out, sort out your feelings, and know all the answers right away.

Your biggest question is probably, *How will I do this on my own?* The answer is: you won't be alone. You can use the coming months to build your support system. You could have family come to be with you or invite a close friend to be with you during delivery. You can hire a doula or birth coach to help you stay calm and look out for your medical needs. You can join supportive groups or clubs for moms, either at the gym, your faith community, or in your neighborhood. Numerous outreach programs and services exist to support new parents during deployment. The more you reach out and connect, the more you will realize you don't have to be alone.

For inspiration, consider the behavior of a herd of elephants when one of the females is ready to give birth. The male elephants are usually not around, so the entire herd is females. First, the herd circles around her to protect her during labor. They make a tight barrier so no predators can disturb her. Then, when the calf is born, they become excited and trumpet loudly. The calf is welcomed into a circle of strong, protective females who are there to help it stand for the first time. The support network you build now, during pregnancy, will become your herd of elephants. Seek out the people you want to circle around you and support you during the birth.

Many military spouses have been in your shoes before, and every one of them discovered strength they didn't know they had. It feels intimidating now, but you do have the strength and courage to get through this pregnancy and birth. When you do, you will feel so incredibly proud of yourself, and best of all, you will have a beautiful new baby to love. You will also become part of an exclusive group— one you can only join by having a baby during deployment. It's a close-knit group, one that will always support each other. It may not be a club you are eager to join, but here you are. You can be a proud member, and we are eager to help you through.

Giving birth during deployment is not ideal, of course, but it is possible. Instead of wishing things were different, focus on anything that helps you feel calmer about the birth. When faced with a large, overwhelming challenge, many people find comfort in focusing on smaller details that are within their control. Something that will help you feel confident and less stressed is planning and preparation.

If this is not your first baby, start by making arrangements for who will stay with your other children when you go to the hospital. Is it practical for your parents or a sibling to come? If not, find a friend nearby who can be on call when your due date is near. Have a plan for daytime and nighttime. Who will pick up the kids if you go into labor during the school day, or stay at night when they are asleep? Have a backup plan in case of illness. You will feel calmer when labor begins.

Plan with your service member how you will communicate during the birth. They may be able to participate in the birth remotely, via phone or video. The military chain of command usually tries to assist as much as possible. Your service member's communication options will vary greatly depending on their location in the world, military branch, and electronics available. Practice communicating with different methods ahead of time to see what works best.

Every situation is different, so don't expect your deployment birth story to be like someone else's experience. Sometimes the military is able to send a deployed service member home in time for a birth, but do not expect it or count on it. It depends on the service member's job, location, and where the birth falls in the deployment cycle. Even with the best intentions, travel plans are often made on very short notice, and your baby's due date can change, even if you have a scheduled delivery. It is best to be prepared for a delivery without your spouse.

Your service member will probably be in touch with you and know when you are getting close to delivery. You can also contact your unit liaison to relay a message quickly to your spouse's chain of command. Knowing that you have options to get in touch with them can bring a sense of relief.

Even with these channels in place, plan to send a Red Cross message as soon as you are admitted to the hospital. A Red Cross message is an important official step necessary to verify your medical situation. That verification may be required to allow your service member special privileges such as communicating with you remotely during the birth of your baby. A Red Cross message is used to verify any emergency notifications such as a premature delivery. After you are admitted, you can initiate this process by calling the Red Cross. A representative will speak briefly to an admitting doctor or nurse to verify your status as a patient. You will be required to provide your service member's full name, rank, service branch, social security number, unit address and the address of the deployment location. Be sure to collect this information and take it with you to the hospital, along with the Red Cross phone number for emergency communications.

Make a birth plan and decide who you want to support you in the absence of your spouse. You need an advocate to be with you, such as a family member, friend, or birth coach. During the birth, you may have to make decisions for yourself and your baby. No matter how you give birth, you will experience some pain and discomfort. You will want someone to hold your hand and calm you down, bring down your heart rate, and help you manage pain. Ideally, you should choose a close friend who has given birth before, makes you feel relaxed, is not squeamish, and has a good sense of humor. Even if you have a good friend who doesn't quite fit all those qualifications, go ahead and ask anyway. Having someone there is better than being alone.

Another option is to hire a doula, a professional birth coach who will be there to support and defend you. They are most often used for natural births, but a doula can be useful to support any birth plan, from admittance to delivery and beyond. A doula has medical training, so they can ask the doctor questions, help you make informed decisions, and voice your wishes when you can't or when you need reinforcements. One way or another, you will benefit from having an advocate by your side, whether a family member, friend, or professional birth coach.

If you are going to give birth during a deployment, it's okay to feel scared and intimidated, but you are not alone. Surround yourself with people who love and support you—your protective circle of elephants. Lean on other military spouses. Be inspired by their experiences. If you take time to plan and prepare, you will gain the peace and confidence to face the challenge ahead. You are stronger than you know. You can do this!

Open When

You're Thinking About
Relocating During Deployment

Dear Decision-Maker,

Your service member will be deployed for several months, maybe as long as a year, and you are wondering where you should live while they are gone. After all, you are probably living where you are because of your spouse's duty assignment. Now you're free to move about the country, right?

Of course, you don't have to go anywhere. Your service member will continue to receive a housing allowance for your home during deployment. If you live in military housing, you can remain there. In fact, wherever you live, you can stay right where you are.

However, relocating might be appealing to you for various reasons. Maybe you just don't feel connected and supported where you are. You might want to be closer to extended family. Your reasons might be financial, if you hope to save money by living with your parents, moving to a smaller place, or moving in with a friend.

No one can decide for you where you should live during deployment. Yes, this even includes your service member. While you value their opinion and want to take it seriously, in the end they will be gone, and you will be the one who has to deal with the living situation. Ultimately, you should choose to live where you have the best support and the least conflict. That place is different for everyone. Take the time to decide what is best for you in your current state of life, and remember, what worked for someone else may not be the best choice for you.

Where you choose to live will have a huge impact on your quality of life during deployment. Think first about your personality and what is most important to you during this time. Do you plan to focus on your job or taking classes? Are you happiest when you have friends nearby and social plans every weekend? Are your family relationships strained with drama and arguments? The answers can help you decide what will be the healthiest environment for you in the months ahead.

If your parents or family are supportive and you need help with small children, living with or near extended family might be the way to go. Or perhaps there is another compelling reason to be near your family at this particular time. You may want to be back in your hometown instead of being by yourself for the lonely months of deployment. That's understandable.

If you decide to relocate, even for very good reasons, be sure the benefits outweigh the difficulties of moving. If you have children in school, is it worth adding a move, school change, and leaving friends on top of the stress of deployment?

If you have a job you enjoy or need, will it be hard to find another one? How could relocating affect your access to health care?

Can you handle living near your parents or in-laws, or with them? Some people love having the extra company, while others who move home feel frustrated living in someone else's space. If you have children, you have your own rules and ways of parenting. If you decide to move in with family, have plenty of open discussions ahead of time about sharing expenses and household responsibilities. Even if you are not living with family but nearby, you may need to establish rules and healthy boundaries to be sure your family recognizes and respects you as an adult and the parent of your children.

You should realize going back home will be different than when you lived there before. Many of your friends will have moved away. Your parents' lives will have changed. Perhaps they spend more time at work or with friends than they used to. And if you are the only military-connected person in town, you might feel very alone in your deployment experience. Be realistic about the pros and cons of relocating, no matter where you go.

Deciding where to live during deployment can be a difficult choice, but it is one you need to consider carefully. Stand up for what is important to your own physical, mental, and financial well-being. The right choice for you during one deployment may not be the same for the next deployment. When your life changes, so does the equation. For every deployment, take all the circumstances into consideration. Take your time, and decide what is best for you. Wherever you choose to live, make the most of it!

Open When

Pre-Deployment Trainings
Exhaust You

Dear Tired Friend,

You were expecting deployment to be hard but you're already exhausted, and this deployment hasn't even started! You are probably realizing all the trainings and workups your spouse has to do in the months leading up to deployment are an ordeal unto themselves. Perhaps it feels as if the pre-deployment stage is more stressful and frustrating than the actual deployment. If you're feeling worn out and wondering how to get through the months ahead, you're not alone.

The problem with shorter trainings and workups is they catch you by surprise. The dates for training are on the calendar, but you don't do much to prepare. After all, a week or two or even a month without your spouse shouldn't be a big deal, right? Not compared to the huge deployment looming over your head.

That's where a short training or a series of short absences catch you off guard and turn your world upside down.

Is that where you are right now?

Maybe your service member has only been gone a few days, and things are going wrong all over the place, and you're wondering how you can possibly survive a long deployment if a week-long training feels like this.

Maybe you are feeling stressed because there is so much to do before deployment, and you can't do any of it because your service member is already gone all the time.

Maybe your heart is breaking because the kids already miss their parent. Your service member is gone for a week, back for a week, then gone for a month. The kids are confused, already acting out, and you are frustrated. Maybe you wonder why you are crying and emotional when deployment hasn't even started.

It's not just you. This period before deployments is a roller coaster. It often feels like the slow climb up a steep track, where the car is clicking beneath your feet, and everyone holds their breath in anticipation of the enormous drop ahead. Even seasoned spouses will tell you they sometimes find shorter trainings worse than deployment. Your spouse is gone, then home, then gone again. Your emotions are all over the place, you don't feel prepared, and it just makes the looming threat of the long absence of deployment feel that much more insurmountable.

But there is hope. Think of this pre-deployment period as a training cycle for you too. It's a time to learn what works for you and what doesn't when your service member is away. You can practice how to handle challenging situations without them and develop the support systems around you. Every day you are proving to yourself you have what it takes. Even if the house is a mess and the kids are acting out, at the end of the day you have kept everyone alive and held the family together. You are showing you have the strength to keep going, one day at a time.

This may be surprising, but there are some parts of deployment that will be easier than the training cycle. When deployment begins, you will settle into a routine for the long haul. You will be done with the ups and downs of pre-deployment preparation: the errands you are running right now, the hoops you are jumping through, and paperwork you are filling out. When deployment begins, you can focus more on creating the best routine for you.

If you're new to a duty station or haven't made friends yet, now is the time to do it. Look for others who may be going through this same pre-deployment madness and looking for friends. Invite someone out for coffee or to go to a local spouse club meeting. Start making social plans, activities you can look forward to during deployment.

Don't forget to take care of yourself. These workups can wear you down and exhaust you. Now is a good time to establish good self-care habits to take you through deployment. Whether that is an occasional glass of wine, long bath, writing in a journal, phone call with a friend, or extra time at the gym, find what helps you get through.

When workups or trainings are exhausting, don't be discouraged. Consider it a training ground to get you in shape for the long haul of deployment. These days will reveal your areas of challenge, but also show you where you are strong. Take notes, ask questions, learn to laugh at yourself, and hang in there!

Open When
You Don't Understand
Why You're Arguing

Dear Disoriented Friend,

Sometimes preparing for deployment feels worse than deployment itself because of all the accompanying emotions and pressure. These can emerge in bickering or arguing, sometimes over trivialities, sometimes over serious issues. If this is happening to you, don't be alarmed.

The pre-deployment stage is stressful and frustrating for you and your loved one. There are many major decisions to be made, including hot-button issues such as how to manage the budget, deal with your kids—and maybe your parents too—or even where you will live during deployment. Add in the reality check of updating wills, emergency contacts, and other life-and-death considerations, and you've got plenty of material for conflict. With so many decisions to make, it's essential for you each to communicate your opinions and listen to the other person's perspective too.

Sometimes the whole situation feels like a hectic, rushed whirlwind. You might be so preoccupied with all the details and to-do lists that you don't have time to think about being apart. It may even be a welcome distraction from the separation you are dreading.

Other times, the long, painful goodbye of deployment prep seems to drag on way too long. You may both be ready to rip off the Band-Aid and get this deployment started already. You may look forward to departure, simply because it means you can finally start the countdown to when this whole thing will be over.

Meanwhile, you may fight over anything from car maintenance to sandwich condiments. Trivial arguments are doubly hurtful. Not only does it increase tension between you and your service member, but it can also make you feel guilty. You want to treasure your time together before deployment, but instead you go to bed angry because you wanted mustard and got mayonnaise.

Fighting and arguing before deployment doesn't mean your relationship is in jeopardy or that your service member loves you any less. You are both stressed and letting your ugly side show, but it doesn't mean you don't love each other. In fact, venting your emotions to each other is a positive sign. It means you trust each other enough to be vulnerable and honest. You are leaning on each other to get through this difficult situation. Sometimes when one person leans, the other person pushes back, and it creates friction. That's not necessarily a bad thing, but it would be great if it didn't come with all that shouting and crying, right?

You may be surprised and frustrated by your service member's attitude about leaving you. As deployment approaches, they begin to focus on the mission ahead and may seem emotionally detached while you may want to cling to them and savor every moment together. You may feel angry because you feel ignored. You may also be angry at the military for putting you in this position.

Sometimes before deployment, when you and your service member are about to be separated, you might push each other away. This can happen with either you or your service member, and it isn't always on purpose. It may be a subconscious defense mechanism, where one or both of you are trying to make your life together miserable, so it won't hurt as much when you are apart. Of course, there's no real value to picking fights, but it is a common reaction in the time leading up to a deployment. It doesn't mean you are headed for divorce. It means you are reacting like many other military couples do when facing a long separation.

You can reduce your conflict by trying to see your service member's perspective. Naturally, they are focused on their mission and leaning into the task ahead. Of course, they wish they could spend more time with you, but they are also eager to use the skills they've worked hard to develop. Deployment isn't a punishment for you or your service member. It is the culmination of their military training. The mission is one of the reasons your loved one chose this career. When you realize this, it may help you understand why your service member is obsessed with their packing list. They aren't trying to neglect you on purpose. They are simply trying to be as prepared as possible for the mission.

Your service member is probably struggling with the separation too, even if it doesn't seem that way. They feel the same fear, loneliness, worry, uncertainty, and longing as you, whether they express it or not. They may also feel some guilt about their mission focus and about being apart from you. At the same time, they know they have to move forward. They are trained to remain focused on their mission, regardless of their personal feelings. That is why many service members become outwardly detached or distant before deployment. It isn't your fault. It's training. Don't take it as an insult or an indication of trouble in your relationship. It may be helpful for you to talk to someone—another military spouse or significant other—who has been there and can encourage you by sharing their own experiences.

You can also help your service member understand your perspective too. When you find yourself stuck in a rut of trivial arguments, take a step back and evaluate your own feelings, so you can voice them coherently. If you are feeling angry, are you truly angry at your loved one, or are you angry with the military, the deployment, and the general situation? It's okay to be angry; but picking fights with your service member won't help. Instead of directing your anger at your loved one, find ways to express the real sources of your frustration. If you are feeling worried, pinpoint your major concerns. Discuss your fears and worries together. Even if you can't resolve your fears, communicating about your deeper concerns will be more helpful than fighting.

Just because you are fighting now doesn't mean the entire deployment will go this way. Tensions are highest right before departure. You will probably feel a sense of calm or relief after the deployment begins. If you do, don't feel guilty. It doesn't mean you don't love or miss your service member. Your emotions are simply tired of being stretched and held taut. Departure is a release, when the event you've been preparing for is finally happening. After departure, you may be able to resume a more regular schedule, which will relieve some of the tension you're experiencing now.

If you are caught in conflict right now, be encouraged. It won't last forever, and it's not the end of your love. Give your service member and yourself some grace and forgiveness. Do what you can to lower the tension level and find healthy ways of expressing your emotions. You and your service member can get through this and become stronger together, even while you are apart.

Open When
It's Time to Say Goodbye

Dear One Left Behind,

Now your service member is going through all their gear, preparing to roll up their uniforms and pack them up. Seeing their gear spread out all over the floor is an emotional experience. On one hand, you may be ready to be done with the emotional tightrope leading up to departure. On the other hand, you're grieving over the coming departure and all the "lasts" you are experiencing—the final Sunday together, the last dinner at a favorite restaurant, the last family movie night, the last morning waking up together.

Savor those memories and store up every little detail. Take pictures and make little videos of those everyday moments so you'll have them to look at during deployment. Don't wait to take pictures on the last day, because those moments will be hectic and full of last-minute details. Take photos whenever you think about it, here and there throughout the last week or so.

Eventually, the gear will be packed, the alarms will be set, and the dreaded day will come. They have to leave, and you have to let them go. It is just as difficult for your service member as it is for you. Don't make it more difficult for them with last-minute pleas for them to stay or demands to repeat promises they have already made.

You may not want to cry in front of your loved one, but let's be real—almost everyone is going to cry at some point that day. It doesn't matter if you hold back your tears or not. You're both going to feel the pain of separation, so do whatever feels more natural to you. Cry together or smile bravely when you wave goodbye and cry on your way home or after the kids are in bed.

Maybe you are concerned because you don't feel like crying at all on departure day. Instead you are numb. Departure can be so overwhelmingly sad that your brain may shut down some of your responses. If this happens to you, give yourself time. Your feelings will reawaken, and the tears will come eventually, even if it takes a day or a week. You may feel like you are waiting for the reality of the deployment to hit you, because it doesn't feel real at first. Don't worry or feel guilty if you aren't crying. Everyone processes separation in their own ways.

The most important thing about saying goodbye is expressing how much you love each other. It is painful to be apart, but your love is strong. That strength will carry you through situations that feel almost impossible to you right now. Even though it hurts, even though you don't feel ready, and even though you wish you could do anything to keep your loved one with you, remember your love, and remind each other how strong your love is.

Before departure, think about what you will do afterward, particularly if your service member leaves early in the day. You may want to throw yourself into work or school, to get back into a routine as soon as possible. Or you might prefer to take a day off to have time to process your emotions or to cry all day if you feel like it. You might want to spend time with one friend or several. You might indulge in a special meal or dessert, or you might have no appetite at all.

Talk to a friend ahead of time who can be on call for you in case you are overwhelmed while eating dinner alone the first night or two. If it will help you, make plans with a friend and have the glimmer of a fun event to hold onto and look forward to after departure. Have coffee or dinner. Go out for ice cream, a movie, or do some shopping together. Take a hike or a bike ride, a yoga class, whatever is fun and distracting to you. Of course, ice cream and shopping aren't going to make everything magically better for the next few months; but making these plans may help get you through the first days or the first weekend. That's enough to focus on for now.

Sometimes it isn't until you go home and have to sleep in an empty bed that it all becomes real. At home, your loved one's clothes might still be on the floor, their dishes still in the sink. Their damp bath towel is draped over the shower rod in that lopsided way they always leave it. And their side of the bed is so empty and cold. Any or all of these might bring a lump to your throat and make you cry all over again.

Maybe putting your space back in order gives you a sense of peace and purpose, but if you don't have the energy even to clean one thing, that's okay too. You may want to leave some of your service member's belongings where they left them, because it reminds you they still live there. They still belong with you. Before you wash all the laundry, you could set aside some of their clothing. You may find comfort later in having something that smells like your loved one.

Whether you are a whirlwind housecleaner or a binge-watching, binge-eating hot mess during the first few days of deployment, give yourself grace to process this day—and all the days of deployment—in the best way for you.

You may cry all day the first day, and you might cry a little each day they are gone. You may be overwhelmed with your emotions, or you may feel numb. You may want to tackle your to-do list, or you may want to stay in bed. All of these reactions are normal, and you will find ways to put one foot in front of the other and move forward.

After one more hug, one last kiss, it's time for your service member to go. This is the beginning of their mission and yours. Let them go do their work. Keep your head high, because you have important work to do too.

When the goodbyes are over, your countdown to homecoming starts. Here it is: day one of your deployment has finally begun.

Open When

Everything Is Falling Apart

Dear Hot Mess,

So you've had a bad day—or week. Everything is going wrong all at once, as if being on your own during deployment wasn't bad enough. *Why is this happening?* You are carrying a lot on your shoulders already, and now you're feeling you might be at your breaking point.

Call it the Deployment Curse, or call it Murphy's Law. What you're experiencing is common to most military households. If something is going to go wrong, it will happen during deployment. Sometimes it starts the day your service member walks out the door.

Every military family has their horror stories about a deployment disaster. But knowing you're in good company doesn't necessarily make your own mess any easier to handle. Sometimes you're just frozen in place, staring at a mess, and trying to decide whether the best plan of attack is a mop, a roll of paper towels, or a whole pint of ice cream.

There are plenty of times you will want to cry or throw in the towel. Adulting on your own during deployment is hard. When something goes wrong, and you are the only adult in the house to handle it, then it is even more frustrating.

It would be great if there were a foolproof way to avoid this curse. Planning ahead can prevent some problems or at least give you a way to handle some of them. Preventative maintenance on vehicles and appliances may help you avoid the headache of flat tires and broken washing machines. Making a spare key for your house and car could avert a crisis when you lock yourself out, which is almost guaranteed to happen at least once. Taking care of yourself physically and not pushing yourself to exhaustion will help you stay healthier. Knowing your neighbors and having a few friends you can call gives you options and extra hands if you have to make a run to the emergency room.

Unfortunately, all the planning in the world can't prevent every mishap or breakdown. Stuff is going to happen, and when it does you just have to handle each situation as it comes.

It's okay to cry. It's okay to feel overwhelmed. Feel it, then face this new problem and whisper to yourself, "I can do this." Because you can, but there is no rule saying you have to do it by yourself. This is what your support network is for. Evaluate this problem you're facing. Decide who can help and call them. Call the landlord or the housing office. Call a plumber. Call a friend. Break out the tools, bandages, disinfectant, and mops. When you're done, break out the wine or ice cream; then sit down and do the only thing left to do—laugh about it.

Yes, laugh. It's the best magic for warding off the Deployment Curse. Sometimes laughing is really all you can do. Crying and screaming won't fix anything, but laughter will actually make you feel better. So take a picture of the mess, send it to your friends, or share it on social media, if appropriate. Get your friends to laugh with you. Think about the great—or possibly ridiculous—story you now have to tell your service member about your day. It's a story you will probably tell for years to come. Get some mileage out of that situation!

Many military spouses come to view their battle with the Deployment Curse as a badge of honor, and why not? When you are faced with a seemingly impossible situation and you find a way to get through it, you will gain a sense of strength and accomplishment. You've earned it!

Turn these challenges into a positive. Record your deployment accomplishments, either in a notebook or displayed somewhere in your home. Grab a sticky note. Write down the problem you are dealing with right now and stick it on the fridge, on a wall, in a book. When you have dealt with the mess, write down how you did it and stick that note on the wall too! Add another note whenever something breaks down, or you have to handle an unexpected issue on your own. Watch your confidence grow as the notes multiply, a reminder of all the problems you've solved and the craziness you've managed. And the next time something goes wrong—sorry, but this is almost guaranteed to happen—look at your notes and remember you are strong enough to handle this new challenge too.

Open When

You Want to Trust Your Loved One

Dear Struggling Loved One,

Today you are really struggling to trust your service member while they are so far away. Maybe they have made some choices you don't agree with. Maybe there was a series of messages or emails that concerned you. Or maybe they haven't done anything, but you can't shake the nagging doubt creeping into our heart.

Sometimes, even in the strongest and healthiest relationship, couples struggle to trust each other. For military couples, spending so much time apart can put your trust to the test. You may not know much about what your loved one does each day. Sometimes during deployment it feels like they are living another life. Of course you love your service member! But no matter how long you have been together or how strong your relationship is, you may experience doubt or jealousy during deployment.

Your trust issue might be based on previous relationships. If you or your service member have had negative experiences—with someone else or with each other—lingering insecurities can return with a vengeance during deployment. It's difficult to separate the past from the present, especially if you and your service member have had relationship or communication issues. Wondering and questioning and looking for signs of infidelity are common reactions.

As if this weren't bad enough, maybe you've been hearing horror stories from other spouses. There are plenty of stories floating around about service members or spouses cheating during deployment—some true and some not. Some relationships don't hold up to the pressures of deployment, but that doesn't mean yours won't.

Most couples are completely faithful during deployment. Spouses back home are too busy working and taking care of everything to get involved with someone else. Service members overseas are also busy and overworked. If you focus on the horror stories, you will miss the stories of the beautiful couples who wait patiently and faithfully for each other. If your loved one has never given you a reason not to trust them, then dig deep and have faith in them during deployment. Give them the benefit of doubt. Trust first before jumping to conclusions.

If you find yourself in this situation of doubting your loved one and questioning their behavior, decide if your fears are serious enough to discuss with your service member. Are there real circumstances causing concern, or are you worried about hypothetical possibilities? Either way, avoid the temptation to vent to your friends or other spouses in the unit. The issue causing your concern could be a misunderstanding, but if you have already shared it outside your relationship, you can't call those conversations back. First, give your loved one a chance to address your concerns and explain their perspective. Avoid accusations or anger. Calmly ask questions in a nonthreatening way. Let your loved one know you feel hurt or confused by their behavior. Be firm if you think they have crossed a boundary in your relationship. Then listen carefully to their response.

If you accept their explanation, reassure them of your trust for them. Make note of positive changes you can make in the future to help you feel more confident and assured in your relationship. Tell your service member what they could do to help you feel more confident.

If your service member's responses are evasive or cause you to have more questions or concerns, evaluate your responses thoroughly. Perhaps you don't think they are being honest, or you may not be sure what normal behavior is for deployed service members. This is the time to find someone to talk to. A military chaplain or another counselor can help you decide what to do next. Consider whether you may need legal advice or financial assistance. Surround yourself with positive, supportive people if you find yourself in a bad situation. If you choose to talk to trusted friends or family members, be sure they will keep your confidences to themselves.

Before you get to that point, be sure you have a healthy perspective of the situation. The added strain of deployment on a relationship and the limited communication sometimes make it hard to be objective.

Are your emotions getting the better of you? Are your fears just a temporary reaction to this stressful emotional environment? Or is there truly a problematic pattern of behavior? Before you say something to your loved one you might regret or take any serious steps, be honest with yourself and check your own reactions.

Most of the time, doubt and trust issues in a relationship can be worked out with calm and reassuring communication. Sometimes resolution may not be possible until the deployment is over and your loved one is back home. Moving forward will be easier when you remember the reasons you love each other and share those reasons with one another. No couple is immune to the challenges of doubt during deployment. A solid foundation of open communication will provide a strong support to lean on when the going gets tough.

Open When

You Miss a Phone Call

Dear Disappointed,

You just looked at your phone and realized you missed a call from your service member. It's a horrible sinking feeling when the one you love is on the other side of the world, and you miss a precious opportunity for a conversation with them. How could this happen? Maybe you were in a meeting or you were somewhere with poor reception. No matter how or why it happened, it feels like a crushing defeat that can ruin your whole day.

You have too few opportunities to connect with your loved one. You desperately want to hear the voice you love. Whether it has been hours or weeks since you heard from them, your longing is the same. You love them and miss them, so those moments of connection are everything to you.

Missing a call comes with sadness and guilt. You should have turned the ringer up or hurried to get to the phone more quickly. You feel guilty for being with a client or occupied with work when your loved one was trying to call. Or maybe you feel panicked, wondering if they are okay. *What were they calling about? When will they call back? What if they can't?* It's a helpless feeling.

Part of the deployment communication struggle is because it's typically one-way. If the service member calls from a satellite phone or from a Wi-Fi hotspot, there may be no way for you to return the missed call. In a world where we have an array of technology at our fingertips, being unable to talk to your loved one seems unthinkable.

Plan with your service member to make and receive phone calls at times that work for both of you as much as possible. Find ways to keep track of the time difference between your locations. Every couple needs time to connect, but every individual also needs time to work and rest.

Sometimes, calls happen on a schedule neither of you can control or predict. To be ready for calls at any time, charge your phone at a regular time each day. Turn the ringer up or use a smart watch to notify you of calls when your phone is not with you. Explain to coworkers or your supervisor the reason you may need to take calls at odd times.

If you are struggling after a missed call, give your loved one a chance to call again. If you can, take a break from what you're doing, find a quiet place with limited distractions, and take a few minutes to collect your thoughts. If the call doesn't come, use the extra time for positive thoughts or a prayer.

If they don't call back, allow yourself a few minutes of pity. You miss your service member, and of course you are sad to miss a chance to hear their voice. Then channel your loneliness and disappointment into something more positive. Maybe you can send a text, write an email or a letter. Make a journal entry to sum up how you miss your loved one and why it means so much to hear from them. In whatever way you can, let them know you value their time and love hearing their voice. That way, you are using a negative experience to breathe life into your relationship.

You'll be more than ready for the next call.

Open When
It Seems You Never Get to Talk

Dear Ghosted Loved One,

The beginning of the deployment can be a huge shock to the system. You are used to being with your loved one all the time and talking whenever you need to or texting all day when you are apart. Then suddenly, they are unavailable. You feel like you are always waiting for them call or reply to messages.

Don't interpret the level of communication as a measure of your loved one's commitment to you. Embarking on a deployment is an extremely busy and disconcerting time for your service member. They may travel through several time zones, unload equipment, and work long shifts to get established at a new location. During deployment, the mission is their primary focus. They may not get many opportunities to check in with you. It's not because they don't miss you or aren't interested in your relationship. They are just dealing with the pressure of their duties, challenging environment, and very busy schedule.

Give them time to adjust and figure out their communication options. Communication may be limited by the circumstances of the deployment, such as a remote location, demanding schedule, security concerns, and more.

Time zone differences are another obstacle. Your service member may be on an opposite sleep schedule from you. It can be hard to find a time to talk when you are both fully awake. It might even be difficult to remember what time it is on the other side of the world. Some couples keep an additional clock or watch set to one another's time zones to help them remember their loved one's schedule. Sometimes you may have to talk at inconvenient times, such as the middle of the night for one of you. Be careful about interrupting your sleep schedule on a regular basis, especially if you already struggle with sleep issues during deployment. Of course, you want to make every effort to connect with your service member, but don't weaken your health by staying up every night waiting for a call or message. If possible, schedule calls with your loved one so you know when they are coming, rather than staying awake wondering.

Maybe you are halfway through deployment and you thought you had a good routine for communication. For some reason, your service member has either suddenly stopped replying to messages, or they seem disinterested when you are able to connect. Naturally, you're frustrated, and your mind is spinning with possible causes for this change. Before jumping to conclusions, realize there are many reasons communication could be interrupted or changed.

Your loved one could have had a schedule or a shift change. They may be experiencing a wave of homesickness that only gets worse when they call home. They could be experiencing the mid-deployment sensation of *Groundhog Day*, where they feel as though they are living through the same day again and again, with nothing new or interesting to talk about. Sometimes operational security (OPSEC) concerns severely limit what they can talk about, which adds another layer of difficulty to your communication. If this is the case, and it seems your conversations have become repetitive, try playing a word game or ask each other silly relationship questions. This will provide fresh conversations and a distraction when topics such as your loved one's daily activities and events are off-limits because of OPSEC.

Sometimes deployed military units declare a communications blackout, restricting or shutting down all personal communications. Blackouts happen for different purposes, such as routine training or when service members are involved with a sensitive mission. A blackout also happens when there has been an injury or death in a military unit. The blackout allows time for affected families to be officially notified by the military before anyone else is informed. If your communication has been steady and suddenly goes dark, try not to worry. If anything happens to your service member, you will receive word as soon as possible. All you can do is wait until the blackout is lifted.

If you know other service members from your loved one's unit are still communicating regularly with their families but you are not hearing from your loved one, it's still no cause for alarm. When you have a chance to talk or send a message, don't assume the worst or pressure your service member to answer questions about your relationship or their behavior. Instead, simply reach out and let them know you are there and you continue to support them.

Possibly you have friends who get to talk to their deployed service member almost every day. This makes it harder for you when your communications are more limited or less frequent, but the ability to call home or stay in touch is not the same for every deployed person.

Some deployments simply don't provide many opportunities to communicate. Service members serving on submarines, in special forces units, or in combat locations may have infrequent or unreliable communication options. This could last an entire deployment, or it could just be for a period of time while your service member is on a specific mission or at a particular location.

During a deployment with limited opportunities to communicate, consider keeping a journal or notebook of letters to your loved one. Write while they are gone and exchange letters when the deployment is over to read about each other's experiences. Even if your loved doesn't get to read your words now, being able to write to them can give you a feeling of closeness. You and your loved one can also choose a book to read simultaneously while you're apart. Write about your thoughts and impressions of what you are reading. Even if you can't correspond in real time, you may feel closer because of the shared experience. Save the messages to talk about when you are able to connect or even when deployment is over.

You may also benefit from speaking with a clergyperson or counselor if you are feeling disconnected during deployment. While no one can replace your loved one, there is a definite benefit to having a third party listen and offer support and guidance.

Communication is always a struggle during deployment, for you and your service member. Some individuals are more able to vocalize how they feel and function during deployment than others. Each of you may have to give a little to find a communication solution. Always give your loved one the benefit of the doubt if it seems they are less available or communicative than you would like.

Dry spells or communication limitations during deployment are very common. Whether your communication issues last for a little time or the whole deployment, you are not alone in your frustration or disappointment. The best approach is to be patient and loving, reminding your service member you will be here to support them in every situation.

Open When

You Want to Set Goals

Dear Motivated Friend,

Setting goals for yourself can help you look at deployment in a positive way. Instead of seeing this as a void of time apart from your loved one, you can view it as a time to invest in yourself. Goals can make the time fly by as you mark the successes of each week or month.

Make the most of a difficult situation by challenging yourself with personal goals. Your goals can be short-term—a new objective each month—or long-term—an accomplishment to complete by the end of deployment. Either way, choose goals to motivate you and keep you in a positive frame of mind.

Everyone's deployment journey looks different. Choose goals that reflect where your life is right now. How would you like to grow or change during this deployment? Complete an education program or certification. Save money. Lose five pounds. Start a journal. Run a 5K. Plan healthier meals. Make two new friends.

Whatever you want to accomplish, set well-defined goals and write them down. When goals are too vague, you may end up feeling frustrated instead of accomplished. Set specific and measurable goals. For example, if your goal is to lose five pounds or to fit in a particular pair of jeans, you will know when you get there. If your goal is "to get in shape," you have no definitive way to know when you've met your goal, and you're more likely to get discouraged or give up.

Weight loss can be measured in pounds or inches lost. Classes can be measured with grades. You can chart the amount of money you save, the number of books you read, or the number of miles you run. In what way can you track your deployment goals?

Also set reasonable and achievable goals. It's good to challenge yourself with a goal, but make sure it's one you can realistically accomplish. Before you declare a savings goal, for example, study your budget to be sure it's doable. If you've never run a mile, you probably shouldn't set a goal to run a marathon next month. Be realistic about the amount of time and energy you will be able to devote to a project during a deployment. If you make your goals achievable, you will feel satisfied with your progress instead of discouraged.

Deployment can be tiring, so choose goals that excite you and motivate you. You can only do so much during deployment. Focus your time and energy on goals that are meaningful to you and will give you a sense of accomplishment.

Break down your big deployment goals into smaller, manageable pieces and set timely milestones to spread out your efforts. If you want to read a dozen books during a six-month deployment, set a monthly goal of two books. To beef up your bank account, divide up your total savings goal by the months of deployment and set aside that amount each month. Then you can easily see if you are keeping up or falling behind and make adjustments along the way.

You may not always accomplish everything you set out to do, and that's okay. Deployments certainly have a way of throwing monkey wrenches into your best-laid plans. But when you have specific and measurable goals for your deployment timeline, you are a lot more likely to meet them.

Take some time today to write down your goals. Break them into measurable pieces and decide how you will tackle them. Best of luck with all your deployment goals, I hope they are a continuous source of motivation!

Open When
You'll Be Apart on a Special Occasion

Dear Table for One,

If you have been a military loved one for more than a minute, you have probably missed celebrating at least one holiday with your service member. Even if they haven't deployed since you've been together, they've surely been away for training, field exercises, or some kind of overnight duty. It stings when your service member is away for your birthday or anniversary, because it's a day you would much rather share with them. Sometimes it's even more painful when they miss major holidays such as Thanksgiving, Christmas, or Valentine's Day. You are missing your loved one, and you're surrounded by other people who are joyously celebrating with their loved ones. Your social media pages may be filled with images of families gathered around festive dining room tables or couples sharing intimate dinners for two. It's on these days when the ache of missing your loved one will be strong enough to overwhelm you.

There's no good way to get around special occasions or fast forward through them, but you can plan ahead for alternative ways to celebrate and make it easier to cope. Anticipate holiday loneliness and consider what will help you get through it. When you know a special occasion is coming during deployment, begin by considering how you would like to spend the day. You may want to reach out to a group of friends and plan something together on the upcoming date. You might prefer an outing on your own to go shopping, to a museum, or to a spa. If possible, you may want to spend it with extended family.

Or you may prefer to spend the day snuggled on the couch, taking some time to rest and recharge. If that's what you need, then make it something to look forward to. Stock up on your favorite snacks and beverages. Light a candle and grab some bath oil for a relaxing soak in the tub. Choose a movie or show you've been wanting to see—

whatever sounds good to you. Find a way to mark the occasion with your own personal celebration. Taking the initiative to plan lets you regain a measure of control over the circumstances of deployment. Of course you will still miss your service member. There's no way to avoid it. But plan your own mini-celebration and don't let deployment steal a special occasion from you.

Deployment may mean celebrating a holiday on your own for the first time, especially if you are not able to travel to family. When this happens, you're in the perfect position to discover this important truth of military life: your military friends become like family. Many other military spouses and significant others are separated from their relatives at the holidays too. They handle the separation by bonding with those who are geographically closest to them and who understand military life.

Plan a casual, kid-friendly potluck with friends who also have deployed loved ones. No one has to do all the cooking, and you can all enjoy each other's company while the kids play together.

Maybe you never considered dining out for Thanksgiving or Christmas, but restaurants and churches around military installations sometimes offer holiday meals for military families, especially those experiencing deployment. You may be hesitant if you don't know anyone, but you will be surprised at the kindness and camaraderie you will find. Bring another military spouse friend with you if you want some company.

Another option is to invite family to come to you. Maybe your siblings or parents are able to visit you. Having even one relative visit during a holiday makes it a special celebration. Don't assume your family knows you are lonely and want them to come. Invite them.

Sending special care packages to your deployed loved one is another way to lift your spirits at the holidays. Get the kids involved and ask family members to contribute something special to the package.

It also may help you to remember you aren't the only one alone or far from family at the holidays. Take a meal or holiday baked goods to single service members in the barracks or dorms. If you are comfortable, invite someone to your home who would otherwise spend the holiday alone. Spend the day volunteering at a local food bank or church outreach. When you focus on the needs of others, you will find your own loneliness melt away.

If you are missing the big family get-together back home, join in by phone or video to see those aunts and uncles and cousins you haven't seen in a while.

Even when you're apart, you can find meaningful ways to mark the holidays. Take the time to think about how you want to celebrate. Think of ways to refresh both you and your service member. Don't be afraid to branch out and create a new tradition or make a new friend. You'll get through this! You and your loved one will celebrate together another year and for many more to come.

Open When
You Have Little Ones Who Need You

Dear Solo Parent,

You are probably tired of people taking a look at your kids, then at you and saying, "You really have your hands full!" At the same time, you're also probably exhausted from, well, really having your hands full. All the time.

Navigating deployment as a parent is an exhausting, never-ending, and thankless task. Even though your service member's job is always demanding, when they're home you can still get an hour of respite or a few minutes to take a shower! Now you never get a single moment's break. It's just you—all you—every moment of every day. It's okay to say it: you are utterly worn out and not sure how to do this.

The truth is, dear parent, you aren't supposed to do this on your own. You and your service member are a team. When they are gone, you shoulder the burden, and it's exhausting to fill the role of two parents. At the same time, you carry the additional burdens of deployment: worry about your service member's safety, lack of communication, and fear of the unknown. Plus all the chores of managing a household. One person simply can't do everything. When your service member isn't there to be your supportive team member, you need to build up your team. You also need to care for yourself, for your own sanity, and also for your children.

I know all the excuses, because I've used them too. *We don't live near family. There's no money for a babysitter. I don't have time to get away. A pedicure sounds really selfish—and besides, my baby gets upset when he's away from me.* Sound familiar? Yes, I lived through those stages of motherhood, not taking care of myself because the kids came first. I pushed and exhausted myself because I wanted to do the best for my children.

However, I learned that doing everything for my children every day without a single break is not what's best for them. As a parent, if you are exhausted, losing your cool over minor problems, or yelling over silly setbacks, you are not doing what's best for them. Children need love and support, which is most effective from a parent who values themselves and gets a break sometimes. If you are emotionally drained, you have little to give. The old saying is true: you can't pour from an empty cup. You are a parent, but you are a person first, and you need to take care of yourself before you can truly take care of others.

When you are raising little ones on your own during deployment, you need a support team. Parenting is challenging. When you are tired during the day and getting interrupted sleep at night, everything is more frustrating. And sometimes when you see the rest of the day full of nothing but feeding little people and changing diapers, it feels as though you're losing a little bit of yourself. Every solo parent has those thoughts, even though they love their children dearly.

There will be days where you simply can't do it on your own, and it takes a strong parent to admit that. I hereby give you permission to share the burden and ask for help. Turn to fellow parents in a play group or a friend or neighbor, or hire a babysitter. Ask someone to watch the kids while you go to a doctor's appointment or the commissary. Use your local YMCA for two hours of onsite childcare while you walk on the treadmill, swim in the pool, or just relax in a quiet place. The child development center on your installation might offer a deployed parents' night out. You can use that time to get together with friends, clean your house in peace, or enjoy takeout at home by yourself. Above all, I want you to do it without guilt.

Those moments of self-care will refresh you and give you courage for the long days ahead. You'll have more strength to get through the hard moments and more creativity to manage each day as it comes. When you build a team, you'll have a network of support, friends you can call on when you are juggling too much and get overwhelmed.

You may think self-care only refers to spa days, mimosas, or vacations, a luxury you simply don't have time and money for right now. But caring for yourself is not a luxury. It is essential. Self-care can be anything you enjoy: taking a long bath when the kids are in bed, listening to an audiobook or podcast, going for a walk, putting the kids to bed early. Self-care means taking care of yourself, physically and mentally. It's not optional. It's absolutely important for every parent, including you.

You are a great parent—even on your tired days, your bad days, and the moments you lose your temper. You love your children, and you are doing your best for them. But there's no prize for suffering or taking on too much during deployment. Only exhaustion and discouragement. When you are struggling, something has to give, and that shouldn't be your sleep or your mental health. Instead, cut back on your workload and simplify some of the tasks around the house.

Allow yourself to create some helpful shortcuts. Yes, it's okay to serve cereal or sandwiches for dinner sometimes. Maybe even ice cream, occasionally. Of course, your children will survive eating from paper plates. Yes, grocery delivery is worth it; and hiring help for housecleaning and yard maintenance is reasonable. You can't put a price on sanity, so anything that saves your sanity during deployment is totally worth it!

Sometimes just an hour is enough time to regroup and go back into the grind of diaper duty with refreshed energy. Your children may not be old enough to thank you, but they will notice the difference at home between an exhausted parent and a refreshed one.

A marathon runner doesn't push through a whole race without water. Instead they pace themselves, and occasionally stop to rehydrate or eat. In the same way, you need to find the routines, habits, and people to refresh you and help you do your best. You are invaluable to your family, so don't forget that caring for them includes caring for you!

Open When
The Kids Are Acting Out

Dear Parent on the Brink,

Every child handles deployment stress in their own way. Some children become quiet and reserved; others begin to throw tantrums all day. It's common for young children to regress and forget skills they have already learned, such as potty-training and sleeping on their own. Your previously sweet-tempered child may transform into a terror at school, or your happy preschooler may now spend each evening crying at bedtime. All these behaviors are normal during deployment, but none of them are easy to deal with.

If your child begins acting out or having troubling behavior during deployment, it can be extremely frustrating. It's particularly exhausting if you are a solo parent trying to meet everyone's emotional needs. You may experience one of those breakdown parenting moments, where you don't know what else to do and feel like a failure. The breaking point can come during a long day of toddler tantrums, or it may hit after months of your teen's sarcastic attitude. Whatever it is that sets you off, you are certainly not the first parent to feel like your kids are going wild and taking you with them.

Deployments are overwhelming for kids of any age, from toddlers to teens. Young children may not be able to understand a parent's absence or the passage of time. Older children become more aware of their parent's absence and the danger they may face during deployment. Even if your child has been through deployment before, they have grown and changed since then, so they may face a new set of challenges this time.

Children experience most of the same deployment emotions as adults, but children may not be equipped with coping strategies or the words to express themselves. They may act out because they are unable to process the loneliness, fear, insecurity, or anxiety they feel. Instead they may channel their stress into negative behavior. This is not because you are a bad parent. Let go of that guilt hanging over your head and realize it's not your fault if your child is acting out or angry. They may be angry at the military and their deployed parent, but because you are the parent they see every day, you bear the brunt of it.

It's a lot for any parent to handle, and you're dealing with it day after day without your partner there. It's okay to ask for help. It's not just you—every parent has these experiences during deployment.

You don't need to know all the answers for your child by yourself. Military families have numerous options for resources to support you and your children during deployment. Reach out for some expert advice to help your family face these challenges.

During deployment or at any time, talking to a counselor about what you and your child are going through will give you actionable steps to manage stress, effectively talk with your child, and determine if your child's behavior needs further attention. As a military family, you have several options for any counseling or mental healthcare you may need. You can get more information from your family center or online.

If parenting during deployment is wearing you down, please know you are not the only parent who feels that way! Use the resources available to you to gain confidence as a parent and also help your child deal with all the emotions they are experiencing. Taking a step back and getting some outside perspective can help you sort it out. You may be a solo parent temporarily, but you do not have to go through this challenge alone.

You Hit the Deployment Wall

Dear Had Enough of This,

It's happened. You've reached your limit. Maybe you've had a really bad day or series of bad days. Or maybe this feeling came out of nowhere when you thought you were doing just fine. You might be at the beginning of deployment or at the end, but one thing is for sure—you don't know how you can handle one more day of this.

Anyone who has been through deployment knows and understands where you are right now. When the days feel endless, you are completely out of energy, and you just don't know how you can do it anymore. It doesn't matter how many deployments you've been through before, or how strong and capable you are. Of course you are strong. You are also human, and you have limits. Everyone does. During deployment you are guaranteed to be pushed to those limits at least once, and it can feel like being slammed into a very sturdy and unmoving brick wall. This is the Deployment Wall, and you've hit it.

Deployments are long, and they will challenge you in every possible way. Some days you will want to break down and cry, and sometimes that may be just what you need. The Deployment Wall is there for a reason. It's an indication you need to make some changes, do something different. You are hitting that wall because your mind and body just can't take anymore. You may be exhausted, overworked, and feeling isolated. Listen to your body and your mind. Take care of yourself before tackling any more challenges.

You may hit the wall because you're exhausted. It's hard to get enough sleep when your loved one is in a different time zone, and you never know when they might call. Being away from the most important person in your life is wearing, especially when you are often concerned for their safety and well-being. Find ways to get more sleep and better rest. Limit your social media, especially at bedtime. Turn off the television. Listen to a comforting audiobook or soothing music if you prefer sounds to silence. Get a sitter for the kids and spend some quiet time by yourself or take a nap. Sleep is not optional. It is a necessity. The whole world is easier to handle when you are well-rested.

You may also hit the wall because you have to be everything to everyone. It's hard to be the solo parent when the kids are sick, or sad, or acting out because they miss their deployed parent. It's challenging to handle every problem, run every errand, make every decision, pay every bill. If you are overwhelmed by your responsibilities, ask for help. Get a sitter or trade babysitting with another parent in need of a break. Pay a neighborhood teen to mow the lawn. Ask a friend to come over and hold the baby while you shower and do some laundry. Talk to your boss about changing your work hours if you can. Whatever you need to do, it is okay to cut yourself some slack. Deployment is a huge challenge, but it isn't permanent. You can pick up some of those responsibilities again when it's over.

Isolation is another reason you may hit the Deployment Wall. Feeling alone magnifies all the struggles of deployment, so it's essential to have someone to talk to. Connect with another spouse for a coffee date or a movie night. Plan a phone or video chat with a friend. If you are a parent, connect with other parents and set up play dates. I know you are busy, but taking care of yourself is truly important. Don't hesitate to reach out to a counselor, therapist, chaplain, or other clergyperson. Interaction and connection will help you feel less alone—because you are not alone—and ready to handle the deployment days ahead.

Laughter can help you get past the Deployment Wall. Deployment feels like serious business every day, but there is a lighter side. Look for reasons to laugh. Maybe you don't think something so simple— even silly—can help you. Trust me, it can. When things go wrong, give yourself a moment to find the humor in your situation. This whole situation could be an entertaining and funny story some day; why not make it a reason to laugh today? Laughter heals and gives you a new perspective, and a sense of humor is a powerful tool for tough days.

The Deployment Wall can be a big obstacle, but you can overcome it with a little rest, a helping hand, someone to talk to, and something to laugh about. You are stronger and smarter than this wall and tougher than any deployment. You can find a way to get a boost over the wall or break through it to the other side. Hang in there!

Open When
You're Planning
Post-Deployment Leave

Dear Excited Planner,

The end of deployment is in sight, and you are ready to plan special time to spend with your loved one! After months apart, you want to treasure every hour together and make up for lost time. You may be dreaming about a luxury vacation with the family or a romantic getaway with just the two of you. Hold on, though. Before you plan your way into the sunset, there are some post-deployment realities you need to consider.

Don't plan to hop on a plane with your service member as soon as you pick them up on homecoming day. For one thing, they've just made a long journey to get home, and they probably want a stay there or at least catch their breath before embarking on any more travel.

Also, after returning from deployment your service member will have reports to write, weapons to clean, and equipment to unpack. They may get a day or two off after arriving home and then have to go back to complete these duties before they can take leave.

It is common for service members to be approved to take a couple weeks off after deployment, but the timing and duration of that leave are not guaranteed. Leave has to be approved by your service member's command and will depend on their position, career field, and any classes or training they are required to do after returning from deployment.

Communicate with your service member to get their best estimate of when they will be able to go on leave. Don't purchase plane tickets or make non-refundable reservations until your service member has final approval for their leave dates. Even then, it's probably a good idea to purchase travel insurance in case everything changes at the last minute.

When you are dreaming of a post-deployment vacation, it's vital to communicate with your service member before making plans. Surprise vacations after deployment are generally not a good idea. Your dreams of an ideal way to spend time together after deployment may be completely different from your loved one's dreams. Maybe you want to spend a quiet week in a hotel, but they want to drive back home and visit family. Service members returning from Middle East deployments may not want to see any more sand, so a beach trip might not be ideal. If your loved one spent deployment on a ship, they probably won't appreciate a cruise. Ask your service member what they really want to do during their post-deployment leave. If your dreams are different, find creative ways to compromise.

Also consider your budget together when making post-deployment plans. You may have saved money during deployment, but your service member may have plans to purchase a new vehicle or pay off a credit card. On the other hand, you may have lost money during deployment if you had to quit your job or pay for more childcare. Be sure both of you are aware of the budget before you book a vacation. It's easier to relax and enjoy your time together when you aren't worried about money.

The time after deployment should be a rewarding and relaxing time for both you and your service member. You both have earned it! The more you discuss your ideas openly and listen to each other's needs, the more you will be able to plan a special time to reconnect and enjoy each other. It doesn't really matter what plans you choose. In the end, all that matters is that you will be in the same place, together!

Open When
Family Members Want to
Be at Homecoming

Dear Conflicted Loved One,

Very often, your in-laws and family members want to see their service member as soon as possible after they are back on home soil. Let's be honest, this can be a challenge. Maybe you get along well with your service member's family and don't mind sharing the big day on homecoming. Other times, having extended family present increases the tension and stress during that event. This may be true even if you have a good relationship with everyone in your family.

The decision about whether to include extended family members in homecoming should be up to you and your service member. Take into account all the circumstances. Will there be a public celebration at the homecoming? Do you and your service member want to include the whole family? If they travel from a long distance, can they stay at a hotel, or will they expect to spend time at your home? Are you prepared and willing to have houseguests at that time?

Whether you invite extended family to come may depend on the kind of homecoming it will be. When military homecomings involve a public event, family members, friends, and guests may be invited to attend. Depending on the situation, there may be reporters and camera crews, marching bands, and well-wishers. It's a big celebration. It's natural for parents to feel eager to be part of a big event to welcome home their deployed child. In other situations, service members come home in small groups or even individually. In an intimate setting, perhaps you would prefer to greet your service member alone.

Also consider the logistics. The homecoming date may change several times before your service member actually arrives. If relatives are flying in for homecoming, they could have a frustrating and wasted trip if arrival is delayed. For the first few days after deployment, the service member may still have paperwork to do, equipment to check in, weapons to clean, and other post-deployment duties. They may not get time off until a few weeks after homecoming.

Remember, after months of deployment and possibly several days of travel on the way home, your service member will be tired. They may simply need time to sleep, rest, and recharge, whether they realize it or not. Even if they are eager to spend time with their parents and family members, they simply may not have the energy right now.

If you and your service member are married, your relationship should come first at homecoming. There are many demands on you both during the post-deployment period called reintegration. Homecoming and the following weeks are an important time of readjustment. You and your service member need time to reconnect, reset your communications, and re-establish your relationship.

If you have children, they need time to get used to having two parents at home, and they will want attention from their newly returned parent. If there are other house guests around, all that will be hampered and delayed. Not to mention the challenge of re-establishing your sex life with your in-laws sleeping in the next room!

For all these reasons, it may be better to avoid long family visits at homecoming. If the family lives nearby and can pop in for the ceremony, that's great! They could even spend some time and share a meal with the service member. Then they can leave and give you time and space to reconnect.

Other factors complicate your decision about whether to welcome family to homecoming. You may be less willing to include family members who were disconnected and unsupportive during deployment. If your relatives have been a source of drama during deployment—or anytime—it's understandable if you don't want to include them at homecoming, especially as houseguests. Your service member may be eager to see their parents or other relatives, but you may feel hurt or insulted by their attitudes during the deployment. At an appropriate time, let your service member know about your feelings and reasons for not wanting their family to come.

If your service member wants their family to come for homecoming, but you don't, you will need to have a very honest conversation. Listen to your service member's heartfelt reasons for inviting family. Communicate your feelings calmly and clearly, so they know your feelings and concerns. Suggest some compromises and middle ground. If you do end up inviting their family, remember it's only for a few days. You will have your service member forever. Even if it's not ideal, waiting a few extra days to get back into a normal routine is not the end of the world. You may have your differences, but your service member's family loves them, and they have also been waiting to see their hero. Be generous for the sake of your loved one. Putting up with prickly relatives can be a thoughtful homecoming gift to welcome your service member home. Discuss the visit ahead of time, make sure you two are on the same page, and set any boundaries necessary for everyone's sanity.

If your in-laws want to be present for homecoming, but neither you nor your service member want them to come, you need to be united when you express your wishes to family. Let your service member break the news to their own parents—and vice-versa—to avoid blame falling on one or the other of you. You and your loved one are a team and must support each other. Be clear, firm, and kind. Establish boundaries and stick to them.

Even if you get along great with all your family and your in-laws, it might be less stressful to invite extended family to come and celebrate a few weeks after homecoming, perhaps when your service member is on leave. If you still don't feel prepared to have a house full of guests, let everyone know up front to avoid miscommunication or hurt feelings.

Sometimes there will be hurt feelings in spite of your very best efforts and plans. Don't let anyone take you on a guilt trip after the long deployment journey you have just completed. You need to choose what is best for your service member and for the health of your relationship and your family as you begin reintegration.

Open When
It's Almost Time for Homecoming

Dear One in the Home Stretch,

You're so close to the end of deployment. You may expect this to be the easiest and most exciting part. You should be jumping up and down for joy, but maybe you're not quite feeling it. It's okay. Give yourself some breathing room. The end of deployment can be just as mind-bending as the beginning. And by this point you might just be too exhausted to be excited. Remember that roller coaster ride during the pre-deployment stage, when it felt like it was clicking slowly up the hill? Now that you have been flipped upside down and taken through all the sharp turns, you just want this ride to be over.

You've been in your deployment mode for months now. You found your rhythm and your routine. You may not even realize all the burdens you are carrying day to day, because these challenges have become your new normal.

When it's almost time to lay some of your burden down, it may only emphasize just how heavy it has become—and you're not there yet. Soon you won't have to sleep alone, pay every bill, and take care of every household responsibility all by yourself. But that time isn't here yet. The final weeks seem to go on forever. Even with the finish line in sight, you may lack the energy to drag yourself across it.

The end of deployment doesn't always come with an automatic sense of euphoria. It comes with uncertainty about being a couple or a family again and plenty of hard work and preparation for homecoming day and the days that follow.

You may have questions and concerns. Will life go back to normal after deployment? Will we be able to pick up where we left off, or will it take a while to get used to each other again? Whether this is your first deployment or your tenth, those butterflies in your stomach will probably be there. How might your loved one be different when they come home? How will they react to any changes that happened while they were gone? How will the kids react to them after such a long absence? The longer the deployment and the bigger the potential changes while you're apart, the more stress you may feel at the end.

You can't avoid this uncertainty when it's time to reunite, but you can rest in the assurance of your service member's love for you.

Homecoming is a joyous occasion, but the end of deployment is also a big change in your household. Any change causes friction—even happy change, such as having your loved one home again. For one thing, you are about to lose some independence and control over your life. While your loved one is gone, you make own your plans, control your own schedule, watch what you choose on television, make what you want for dinner. When they are home again, you may feel silly or even guilty for missing your independence. Obviously, you are happy your loved one is home and safe, but life is going to look different. It's better to respect your emotions about these changes than to ignore them or stifle them. Your mind and body will react to the stress even if you don't pay attention, so it's better to acknowledge your feelings.

If you have children, they may also feel uncertainty as homecoming draws near, knowing or sensing the coming change. As homecoming approaches, the kids may start acting out. This is really hard to handle when you are feeling wound up and anxious as well. Your children may be going through the same emotional roller coaster you are, but they may lack the words or skills to cope with it. Dig deep for some extra patience in the home stretch. Some craziness is to be expected, and you will get through it.

The final weeks of deployment are often filled with a long list of tasks and chores—and more uncertainty. If deployment is extended, it is disappointing and frustrating. If homecoming happens sooner than expected, you suddenly have a shorter deadline for your to-do list and feel the regret of anything you won't get to finish. Whether homecoming happens on schedule or not, you'll be in a flurry of activity. Because of course the house must be deep cleaned. And the garage must be rearranged. And you must have a new outfit...and make homecoming signs. Right?

Honestly, the service member won't care about most of those details. When they first come home, they will most likely be tired and jet lagged. They probably don't want a party, at least not right away. Most service members want a shower, a nap, and a real meal in their own home. Don't worry about getting the house perfect. Instead, focus on making sure they feel at home there. Stock up on their favorite foods and snacks. Make room for them again on the bathroom counter and other shared spaces.

As deployment comes to an end, you may be disappointed or frustrated with yourself if you didn't accomplish everything you had hoped. You didn't lose twenty pounds, finish your degree, or learn a new language. Heck, you never even hung that picture in the hallway. Instead of staying up all night to finish painting the dining room, take a moment to realize none of those tasks had to happen during deployment. And your service member will probably not be focused on any of them anyway. Life will go on, and you will have time to complete those things later.

Instead of worrying about what you wish you had done, focus on what you have done: you made it through deployment. You probably overcame a lot of obstacles to get here. You took care of car maintenance, helped a friend in need, kept your sanity, comforted your children. All these accomplishments and many more. You did it, and you have so much to be proud of.

Don't be discouraged. Face your fears and insecurities. Set reasonable expectations and give yourself time to adjust. It may help you to talk to another military spouse about how you feel. Chances are good they are feeling the same, or they've been there before.

Be patient with yourself and everyone around you. You've each got your own challenges and heightened stress levels as you approach the end of deployment. Hang in there until the end. Even if you have to drag yourself to the finish line, you will get there, and your loved one will be home!

Open When
The Road to Reintegration Is Bumpy

Dear Weary Traveler,

You made it through deployment and your loved one is home! I am so happy for you! No doubt you are happy for yourself. But maybe in the midst of your joy and excitement, you have some questions and concerns: *When will life return to normal? Will your relationship ever be the same again?*

The cycle of deployment does not end at homecoming. Homecoming day is an exciting time. You rejoice to welcome your loved one home. However, that happy day is followed by many days, weeks, even months of adjustment, as the service member rejoins the life of your family and community. This adjustment period is called reintegration. Like deployment, it comes with its own challenges.

Before deployment, you spent a lot of time in preparation. At the end of deployment, perhaps you planned and prepared for homecoming day. You and your spouse should prepare just as much for what happens the next day and all the days of reintegration. How will you bring your lives together again? How will you strengthen and deepen your marriage now that deployment is over?

Both you and your service member have changed during deployment, and your relationship may never be exactly the way it was before. Some of those changes will be for the better. Both of you have grown. You've had unique experiences while you were apart—both good and bad. You have lived through them separately, and neither of you knows exactly what the other has been through. You've each developed new ways of thinking and acting as individuals. During reintegration, you will have to find a new way forward together.

Sometimes this process goes smoothly; sometimes it doesn't. It may take you a week or so to get into a routine, or it may take months. It all depends on numerous factors from couple to couple, or even from one deployment to the next. A new baby, moving, new orders, a loss in the family, and other experiences can complicate the process. Sometimes, this time of reintegration may take as long as the time you were apart. Give it as much time as you need. Don't be impatient with yourself or compare the way you feel inside with the way other couples may appear on the outside. Everyone has their own struggles, even if they're not apparent.

With so much time apart to think and dream and plan while your service member was away, you may have imagined your own version of your relationship. It may not bear much resemblance to reality. It's easy to forget the nitty gritty when you are not together every day. When your service member comes home, you may wonder what happened to your fairy tale. Your romantic dreams did not involve dirty laundry everywhere and a garage full of sandy gear. You did not picture your lover exhausted on the couch or absorbed in video games. You wanted to be happy and feel loved, and you are disappointed and frustrated when life doesn't go smoothly. Conflict can occur when your expectations do not match the reality.

Your service member still loves you, but they are still human. For months, they have been immersed in the alternate reality of a deployment location where they were focused on their work and their own needs. It's hard to imagine how different their life has been from the one they have returned to. It will take time for them to get used to having you and the rest of the family in their thought processes and daily life. Cut your service member some slack for a week or two, at least. Give them time to unwind and enjoy some free time. Talk with them honestly about your desire to have them involved in your life again and reintegrated as an active and loving part of the family.

Very likely, you've changed too. You've become more independent. You're used to being in charge of the household and making your own plans, setting your own schedule. During deployment, you probably didn't share all the mundane details of your day with your loved one. As the end of deployment approaches, you can begin to share more to get them up to speed with life at home. This may make it easier for them to jump back on the merry-go-round of family life.

After deployment, it's not unusual for one member of a couple to want to spend a lot of time together, while the other may have trouble adjusting to so much togetherness. This can be true for either you or your service member. What's important is learning to compromise and find a balance that is reassuring to each of you. You love each other, even if the way you express it is different or may have changed while you were apart.

Whether you and your service member reintegrate in healthy ways depends a good deal on your expectations and communication. Share your routines and create new routines together. Include each other and take time apart when necessary. Be sure to talk about what matters most to each of you, especially anything you've added to your life during deployment. This includes new diets, workout routines, activities, and new groups of friends.

Your household finances may have gone through some changes too. It's common to struggle with balancing the budget during reintegration, especially if one member was managing the bills and savings during deployment. The other spouse may not know the financial details and realities. Be clear about how money is being spent and where adjustments need to be made. If this is your service member's first deployment since marriage, this is an especially important topic. Expenses and benefits are very different for a single person who deploys compared to a married one.

If you have children, they may be very possessive of the returning parent. They may want Mom or Dad to do everything they've missed out on—all in one day. Help children manage their expectations without over burdening your service member or disappointing the child. Help your child make a list of everything they want to do with the returning parent. Let them choose one activity per day. Small children especially will have grown and changed during deployment. Help the returning parent recognize the changes and guide them as they learn to navigate the new relationship. Be encouraging and demonstrate confidence in their parenting ability.

If you have a new baby—especially if it's your first—your service member may not know what to do. Don't laugh! You've had time to practice, and they will eventually figure it out. Show them how to bottle-feed, change a diaper, or give a bath. Then step back and let them do it their own way.

Reintegration will have different challenges for every couple, but the best ways to get through it are with patience and open communication. It takes time to adjust. Give your service member all the time and space they need. Make time to sit down and talk openly with them about any awkwardness or challenges you are facing in the relationship. Ask questions. Listen. Be prepared for tough and difficult conversations. You will be glad you had them. Laugh together whenever possible. Remember why you fell in love in the first place! Do something you both enjoy and let yourselves relax and laugh together.

You and your loved one may benefit from talking to a counselor or clergyperson to help you get through this crucial time. Be aware of any symptoms of posttraumatic stress or mental health changes and reactions that may indicate a need for more in-depth counseling or treatment.

It's normal to feel afraid of the unknown and unpredictable. Draw on your strengths and your love for each other to get through. Even if you have changed, you still have each other. Even if you struggle to reconnect, don't give up. If you are only taking baby steps, you are still moving forward. In time, with good communication and patience, you will be able to reconnect and enjoy an even deeper relationship than you had before deployment.

Seasoned Spouses

My Story
Retirement Was Almost in Sight

We almost made it to retirement. The end was in sight, there was light at the end of the tunnel, and we were all counting down the remaining year my husband had left on his military contract. We bought a "forever home" to live closer to family after retirement. He signed up for transition classes and prepared to transfer into a civilian career. And then…

In true military fashion, we got a surprise that wasn't part of our plan. Dan was selected for promotion. He didn't even know he would be eligible that year. While a promotion is an incredible honor, especially near the end of a career, it comes with strings attached. To accept promotion, he was required to have at least twenty-four months on his contract, starting from the date of promotion. In his case, that meant extending past twenty years of service. An extension meant a new set of orders, which would require another PCS move and possibly another deployment.

I couldn't believe it. We had lived in that house just over a year, and now we had to face another move. This was supposed to be his easy non-deployable assignment where he could coast along into retirement. He had earned this. We all had earned it, after years of sacrifices, long distance phone calls, deployment time zones, and time apart. We were enjoying having Dad live in the house and actually spend time at home every night. Our furniture already had dents and scratches from five moves, and we had selected which pieces would fit in our "forever home." Now we would have to go through everything all over again.

It felt both exciting and daunting at the same time. On the one hand, I was incredibly proud of him for achieving a rank he always held in such high esteem. After nineteen years of service, it felt wonderful to see him publicly recognized for his skills and achievements. But on the other hand, I was just so tired. I had recently given birth to baby number five. I certainly did not feel the youthful energy I had experienced during his first promotion so many years earlier. I was tired of moving and making new friends, weary from juggling the kids' emotions at every new assignment, and worn out from handling so much of our home life on my own. The thought of starting all over again was intimidating and exhausting.

We found ourselves in a unique position to military life: for once, we actually had a choice. Technically, he could refuse the promotion, walk away, and keep his original retirement date. For most of our marriage, he had received orders, and then we had figured out a way to make the most of them. For the first time, whatever we accepted would be our choice. We couldn't blame the military a year or so down the road if we experienced hardship and regret. We finally had some power over our fate, but it came with a heavy responsibility.

For weeks, we weighed the value of the decision. Certainly, there were many benefits to the promotion, including increased retirement pay for the rest of his life. But there were other considerations too. Would it be too difficult for the kids to change schools again? Now that I finally had steady work, would I be able to keep my job if he was gone all the time? Could we afford another house while paying a mortgage on the first one? There were so many unknowns. Because this was happening in the middle of the Coronavirus lockdowns, it sometimes felt as if the whole world had paused and everything about the future was one big question mark.

In the end, the financial benefits won out. He accepted the promotion. Our family moved across the country—again—this time during a pandemic. He was lucky to receive a non-deployable assignment doing work he would enjoy. We found a good home in base housing, and renters for our other house. I unpacked boxes, settled the kids into schools, and after months of holding my breath, finally let out a sigh of relief. It all worked out.

When you have gained experience in this military life, it's easy to be lulled into the belief that going through something once will make it easier the next time around. In some ways, that's true. Every time you go through a challenge, you learn from it. Once you have completed a PCS move, you learn from your mistakes and vow not to make them the next time. Once you go through a deployment, you learn about useful resources and the coping strategies that are most helpful to you. Every experience makes you wiser. However, gaining wisdom and experience will never numb your emotions. Military challenges will always be difficult, no matter how many times you have faced them before. Military life taught me to be flexible and challenged me to pivot our plans, but that doesn't mean the process was easy. Moving was still a stressful and arduous task, even though I had done it so many times before. Spending time apart from my husband still makes me lonely. Just because you have carried a burden before does not make it any lighter.

An experienced military spouse is sometimes called a "seasoned spouse" because life has peppered them with wisdom. While not everyone likes the term, it's one I embraced when I decided to call my blog *Seasoned Spouse*. You may not even realize you have become a seasoned spouse. Hey, you don't need to be old to have a variety of military experiences! But if people come to you to ask questions and find a way to navigate military life, then you are a seasoned spouse.

These experienced spouses are often a great source of knowledge and comfort to newer military loved ones. But people sometimes forget that even seasoned spouses are still in the trenches themselves, still navigating military challenges, and still frustrated when the military throws surprises their way. In addition to the regular burdens, these spouses often suffer from the need to wear a mask and hide their struggles. You've been through this before, so it should be easier, right? People expect you to hold it together. You're supposed to be flexible and pivot. So you put on a brave face and wear that false mask. But you sometimes feel like after all your military experience and everything you have learned along the way, this is the loneliest season yet.

If you are a seasoned spouse, I see you. I know how fulfilling and rewarding it can be when you get to help someone solve a problem or make another family's life just a little bit easier. It's exciting when your own trials and experiences can be helpful to others. But I also know that you are so tired. You are exhausted at the thought of going through this all over again. Not another move. Not one more long separation. After all these years, carrying all these weights, you are weary. You wonder if you even have the strength to shoulder the burden of others.

For all my seasoned spouses, this section is for you. I know you don't need answers about military housing. You've lived there! You don't have questions about acronyms. You already know them! You just need to know if you truly have the strength to reach that light at the end of the tunnel. You are so close to the end of military life, but not quite there yet. And I can truly say, I'm right here with you. Some days are easy, while others are harder, but I know we have the strength. I know we can do this and hold our heads high for just a little longer. I'm here, and we are all in this together!

Open When

You're Tired of Military Life

Dear Fed-Up Friend,

Some days you will feel like a superhero rocking the challenges of military life. But not today. Today you are tired of it. Today everything about military life is exhausting. The deployments. The moves. The judgment and misconceptions of people outside the military community. Raising children alone way too much of the time and not being able to talk to your spouse when you want to. You're tired of being asked for your military member's "last four," as if you don't have your own identity.

Yes, military life can wear you out and drag you down. Sometimes even the little things add up. Then there are those life-shattering moments when you learn of a friend's death or meet a military widow. In those moments the weight and cost of military life may seem too much to bear.

If that is you today, I hear you! You handle a lot in the day to day. You sacrifice so much. It's natural to wonder sometimes if it's worth it.

On days like these, go back to the beginning. Before the fifth duty station, before all the deployments, before you were asked to give up your career so your service member could pursue theirs. Back to the very beginning. Why did your service member join the military?

Everyone joins the military for different reasons and at different times. Maybe you were there with your boyfriend or girlfriend at the recruiter's office as I was. Or maybe you didn't meet your spouse until they were already serving. Maybe they were out of the military, and you thought it was behind them, but after you married, they decided to join again. Whenever it happened, they had a reason for signing up.

This life was not designed to punish you—even though it sometimes feels that way. Your service member joined the military for a reason. It's probably a reason you agree with: taking care of the family, serving the country, being part of a larger mission. Think about that reason and cling to it on dark days like this. Your suffering means something. It is for a greater purpose. That purpose may be your children, your family, or your country—whatever motivates you. But keep your focus on that. Finding your reason for military life will become a beacon of hope—a lighthouse to keep you from crashing on the rocks.

If you don't know your reason yet, or you are just too tired to think about it, then you need to rest and refresh yourself. Get some sleep. Don't wear yourself thin trying to do everything. Take a bath or shower and relax. Call or message a friend. Sometimes you just need to vent and get some things off your chest. Whether you call another military spouse or an old friend from back home, talk to someone who gets you, who will let you complain and whine for a while, then lift you up and brighten your spirits. And make sure you eat something. Your body needs nourishment. There's always ice cream. And chocolate.

In other words, allow yourself some time to be sad, gain a little comfort and rest, then start anew tomorrow. Your feelings are real. There's no point pretending to be happy and strong all the time when you're actually frustrated or exhausted. There's no rule saying military families need to wear a happy mask all the time. Take off the mask. Get the frustration out of your system. Military life is frustrating sometimes. It's okay to say so.

Everyone is allowed to have a bad day, but the most important thing is how you recover from it. Don't let a bad day stretch into a bad week. After you acknowledge your frustrations, you need to find your own methods for gathering strength and getting yourself back on track. It helps to be intentional and seek out moments of gratitude for inspiration. Start with that initial reason that led you and your service member down the path to military life. Then pause to consider some of the benefits and blessings that have occurred along the way. Focusing on positive memories and exciting moments will help guide you to a better mental attitude.

If bad days recur frequently or stretch into much longer periods of exhaustion or sadness, talk to your doctor, a counselor, or clergyperson. Various health issues could be in play. Military healthcare and other programs provide several options for care. Don't hesitate to use them.

Meanwhile, you're certainly entitled to a bad day, and don't think you're alone. You're not the only one who gets fed up with military life. Far from it! We all do at one time or another, so give yourself permission to have a bad day. I hope tomorrow will be a better one!

Open When
You're the Seasoned Spouse

Dear Seasoned Spouse,

After years of adventures in this military life, you have had many experiences and learned a lot of lessons along the way. Whether you are feeling seasoned because you have already been through a few moves or deployments, or you earned the title by default because you are one of the older spouses, being a seasoned spouse means that you have conquered some of the major obstacles in military life. You know the acronyms, you can navigate yourself through Tricare insurance paperwork, and you have your own strategies for unpacking boxes or setting up a new home. Now you have a new responsibility: sharing your wisdom with others.

It would be easy to rest on your laurels, to enjoy the support systems you have built up over the years, and to continue using the same resources that have brought you this far. After all, you have earned it! With all you have been through on behalf of your service member, you deserve a break, and maybe a badge of honor. Now that you know all the hacks to make military life easier, why can't you just be left alone to enjoy it?

The truth is, you didn't get where you are today without the help of many other people in the military community. You probably don't even know all the names of the people who have guided you along this journey. There was the spouse from that first assignment who reached out to check on you when you first moved to the area. There was the neighbor who always lent a helping hand to fix things that broke when your service member was away. And don't forget the numerous spouses who shared resources and answered the questions you posted on social media pages. Every answer that helped solve a problem gave you a little bit of the seasoned spouse confidence you have today. Now the cycle continues.

Your experience has grown into compassion that you can now share with other younger or less experienced military loved ones. Think about some of the letters and moments in this book that are most relatable to you. What stands out as essential information to share with incoming families? What experiences from your military journey would you like to share with others? Being a seasoned spouse is an opportunity to answer questions, lend a helping hand, or reach out to a younger spouse who is in the same position you were in just a few years ago. This is your chance to pay it forward and give back to the community that helped you through your own challenges.

How are you expected to give back? That's really up to you. It depends on your personality, your preferences, and your own financial situation. Many experienced spouses volunteer for leadership positions with their local spouse group. You could become a family readiness group (FRG) leader or a fundraising committee member, conduct classes for new spouses, or volunteer to chair the social club. If you don't want regular time commitments, maybe you prefer to be an advocate online. You can follow military spouse social media to answer questions, show support, and point people to relevant resources. Some seasoned spouses love to work with organizations that support the military community. From national programs to small, local nonprofits, there are numerous ways to use your time and talents to further the outreach of a favorite organization. Some of these positions are paid. Ultimately, when it comes to sharing your gifts with the military community, the method and choice belong to you.

If your service member has reached a high rank, there may be a certain level of expectation that you, as their spouse, will get involved in programs for the service members and families at their assignment. Some spouses embrace this leadership position and enjoy organizing community events or activities for families. Others politely tell the military "no thank you" so they can focus on their responsibilities at work or at home. There are no specific rules about leadership roles for seasoned spouses, so you will have to communicate with your service member to find a role that is rewarding to you and the families in your unit. I will say that when we have been assigned to a unit where the commanding officer was not married and no other spouse stepped up, the whole unit suffered. Communication did not pass smoothly to families, many were uninformed of local resources, and there were no group events to improve morale among families. So if your service member is in a leadership role but you don't have the time to volunteer right now, work to find a substitute who can fill that position and keep things running smoothly.

If you do take on a leadership position, I want to thank you on behalf of the military community. You may not get many accolades or receive public gratitude. When you accept such a role, it's important to have realistic expectations. You won't be able to accomplish everything you want, you probably won't like everyone you encounter, and you certainly can't please everyone all the time. On the flip side, helping others can be incredibly rewarding. You will provide essential support and the work you do will improve many lives. On the frustrating days, focus on success stories and moments of fulfillment. Remember that there is only one of you, and you can't be all things to all people. So center your work around your own strengths and skills, then delegate other tasks to someone else who is better equipped for them.

When you are serving others in a leadership position, it's essential to set boundaries and take care of yourself. Instead of letting volunteer work overrun your home life, discuss with your spouse and possibly with the kids how many hours you can spare for other families. The daily or weekly habits that have kept you strong throughout military life will continue to be important when you are a leader. Be sure to nourish yourself physically, emotionally, and intellectually so you can continue to share your seasoned experiences for a long time. The military will always take whatever services you offer, so it's up to you to define your boundaries and decide when to say no.

Military loved ones who are new to military life always have a strong impression of the first seasoned spouses they meet. That impression can be good or bad. If you take the time to listen to families, provide resources, and make an effort to keep people connected during long trainings or deployment, then people will remember you as an essential community-builder. But if you allow a spouse group to become a clique that caters to only a few voices, then you risk creating a sour impression for numerous new families. That reputation may last for years, even when they travel to new assignments. However you choose to give back to the military community as an experienced spouse, focus on ways you can make a positive difference for others. Think about the spouses who made the biggest impact on your experiences, and try to imitate their best qualities. As a seasoned spouse, you are in a position to share a wealth of information with others and help improve the military lives around you. Thank you for your many sacrifices! Now let's find a way to use your voice for good so you can continue to support the community which has given you so much.

Open When

Your Child Leaves the Military Nest

Dear Transitioning Parent,

How did your little one grow up so fast? Only a short while ago they were a toddler trying to stomp around in those huge military boots, or a grade school student running for a hug when your service member came home. And now your baby is somehow old enough to leave the nest and fly away from home, away from your protection.

More than likely, you will be the one flying away, leaving your first baby behind at a new apartment or at college, and it will be hard. It may be even more difficult if you're returning to an overseas assignment, leaving your child alone on a continent. That flight is a long one, but whether you're separated by an ocean or fifty miles, it won't make much difference to your heart. Maybe your child has moved out on their own but is still near you—until you get orders to move to another state or country. Whatever the circumstances, adjusting to being apart from your child takes time and—let's be honest—quite a few tears. Military life may add complications to your child's departure, but it's not an easy process for any parent.

Are they ready for this? After all, there are days when you still have to remind them to do their laundry or brush their teeth. As the parent of a military child, you have additional worries. All your child has ever known is military life. When they leave the military community, will they find the friends and support they need in another way of life? Will they be able to adjust? Your child has grown up in a series of moves, deployments, and changing schools. They have been the new kid plenty of times before. But then they were always with you. They had someone to run to on tough days. Now they have so much to figure out on their own.

You can take comfort in knowing the experiences of military life have prepared them well for this major life change. Your military child has developed resilience with each move, whether it was a hard one or an especially hard one—because there were no easy ones. The life they have lived has made them adaptable. They can also handle new environments and unique situations with confidence born of experience. Being the new kid has taught them a lot about their own identity, their skills, and how to make friends quickly. They have learned to be accepting of others, because they have lived in places and gone to schools where everyone was not exactly like them. Your child has the common traits of most military children: resilience and empathy. All of these qualities and experiences are about to pay off when they make this next big step.

They will miss their military culture as much as any child misses the place they grew up. But this is not the first time they've adapted to a new place and new ways of saying and doing things. They've played on sports teams with local kids, or maybe they were the new kid in middle school. We all know that's not for the faint of heart. They are strong, and they know how to handle themselves. Grown military kids often say their military upbringing prepared them well to handle life's challenges and changes as adults.

Yes, there will be difficult moments, times when your child will feel like a stranger in their new place. They will be homesick, even if their home has moved to another state since they left it. When they come home for holidays or other visits, they'll feel a different kind of homesickness, realizing the house they left is a place they can't return to. And the friends they knew are far away too. This is a unique heartache of military life. It's painful but also serves to bond the relationships of parents and siblings. Home is where the family is.

When your child leaves the military community for the first time, they may have a bit of an identity crisis. Being a military kid is all they have ever known. Who will they be when they begin a life on their own? Prepare them by reminding them of their individual value and their own qualities, talents, and roles. They are a son or a daughter, a sister or a brother. They are a worker, an employee, perhaps a student. They have their own passions, abilities, and interests. Help your child to fully embrace their unique identity, of which being a military kid is only one part. They can be as proud of the field of study or career they have chosen as they were of being a military kid. As a military spouse, you had to recognize your identity, to learn you were more than "just" a dependent. You can guide your child to recognize their identity too.

As the parent, you will need to prepare your heart for this departure as well. You will learn to embrace a new identity as the parent of a young adult, no longer a child. They will always need your love and support but in different ways than before. As your child prepares to leave the military nest, support them by reassuring them of your love and care for them, no matter what. Let them know—even though they are leaving the military community—their family always knows them and loves them for who they truly are. You always helped them to be proud of their service member, when you taught them to stand for the flag or to show respect at military ceremonies. Now tell them you are equally proud of their accomplishments. They too will work hard and do great things, and no matter what goes right or wrong for them, your love for them will never change.

To you, they may always be that little one clutching a "Welcome Home" sign after deployment, but your child has become a full-fledged adult. It's time for them to spread their wings and fly. Their journey may lead them far from military life, but they will never forget their family and the experiences that shaped them into the strong, confident person they are today.

Open When
You're Searching for Your Identity

Dear Not Just a Milspouse,

Military life is often demanding, and sometimes it seems to take much more than it gives. After years as a military spouse, it's common to feel that your own identity and abilities are tied up in your service member's military career.

Maybe you had to change the direction of your career, pivot to a more portable job, or delay some of your dreams. Perhaps you spent some time unemployed or stayed home while raising your kids or pursuing a degree. Or maybe you have a degree that you never really got to use. Maybe you've dedicated countless hours to military programs and activities.

Friend, no matter how much you supported your service member's career or gave up your own goals to help them achieve theirs, your identity is much more than being a military spouse.

You are an individual with your own strengths, skills, and passions. While I certainly hope you have found some ways to share those abilities with the military community, I have also interviewed enough military spouses to know that the harsh reality of military life is that the entire family makes sacrifices to support the service member. Even when military spouses do this willingly and patriotically, it has a lasting impact on their lives and career path.

If that is how you have been feeling lately, I want you to know there is hope. No matter what difficult situations you have been through, there are new opportunities ahead of you. Life is full of surprising twists. We all learn how to navigate our paths, one adventure at a time. If you are struggling to establish your own identity now or wondering what path to take after your service member leaves the military, then I want you to remember these words: strengths, abilities, passions.

To rediscover your own personal identity, first focus on your strengths. These are the core abilities and behaviors that make you unique. If you were to introduce yourself to a new group, what three strengths would you use to describe yourself? These are not hobbies or things you do, necessarily. It's those things that naturally come easily to you, so you gravitate toward them and express them often. Are you strong, forgiving, and creative? Maybe you are patient, love learning, and have a great sense of humor. Your strengths help define the kind of person you are, and who you want to become. Being more aware of your own strengths can help you define your unique identity in a positive light. This is who you are. This is the beautiful combination that you can offer the world. And it has nothing to do with the words "military spouse" or a title on a resume.

After you become more aware of your personal strengths, it's time to focus on your abilities. Understanding your abilities is a crucial step in entering or re-entering the workforce, if your post-military path is leading you there. Many people associate abilities with job descriptions and resume items, but your personal identity goes much deeper than that. Perhaps you are a great listener or good at making friends quickly. Maybe you have always been an excellent baker, crafter, or home decorator. Or you could be a well-organized parent who keeps everyone on schedule. These are abilities that you have developed through your experiences, and they can be applied to a wide variety of jobs. Feeling stuck? Think about some of the abilities that military life teaches most military spouses. PCS moves force you to manage logistics, plan ahead, and get organized. Through moving, you have learned to adapt to new situations and be open-minded when meeting new people. Deployments teach you to be independent, collaborate with a support network, and creatively solve problems. If you volunteered with a spouse team or unit program, you have learned leadership skills, community involvement, and how to be inclusive.

The abilities you learned through your military spouse experience are qualities employers look for in the workplace. Most employers know that they can teach technical skills to a new employee, but it's harder to teach someone to be a good listener or to be more innovative. Employees don't learn cultural acceptance overnight, but a military spouse—especially one who has lived overseas—has had years of practice being immersed in diverse groups of people and living in unfamiliar places. If you are struggling to see what you have to offer the workplace after years of unemployment and resume gaps, focus on these abilities. Start brainstorming jobs that need your skills.

Finally, an important part of your individual identity is your passions. These are your hopes and dreams, the things that excite you. Passions are the projects you would choose to work on if you had unlimited time or money. Has military life provided opportunities to pursue your passions? What are some goals you had when you were younger, before you became a military spouse? What was the reason you originally wanted a certain job or worked toward a particular degree? Do any of those motivations still rest close to your heart? Is there an interest you have pushed into the background because you didn't have enough time, or because your spouse wasn't home consistently enough to make it possible? As you prepare to transition out of military life, begin to focus on these passions again. If you always wanted a certain job or want to finish your degree or certification, work toward that! If you dream of creating a product, buying a house, or launching a business, take your first steps now, even before your service member completes their military career.

Maybe your time as a military spouse has awakened certain passions within you. Are you passionate about a particular law or issue that affects your family? Have you developed passions for helping a specific group of people? Our country needs caring individuals to keep standing up for justice—not just for military families, but for all people. If community activism inspires you, there are numerous organizations that would love to benefit from your experience.

By focusing on your strengths, abilities, and passions, you define your personal identity. You are a unique individual with many gifts to offer. While your experiences as a military spouse may have required a lot of sacrifice and career flexibility, they have also helped shape you into the incredible person you are today!

Open When

It's Time to Leave Active Duty

Dear Nearly Finished,

Congratulations on sticking with your service member through all the ups and downs of military life! You have been through it all together. Now, at long last, you are near the end of your military years. You can see the finish line! Whether your service member is getting out after four years, or they have been in the military for more than twenty years, you are probably feeling a wide range of emotions. In some ways, it's similar to everything you experienced when you first began this military journey. It also requires preparation and planning. You are probably planning the ways you will celebrate this milestone. Be sure you also plan for what comes after it. You and your service member should have detailed and realistic conversations about how retirement will change your employment and financial situation as you prepare to leave active duty.

You must be so excited, feeling a huge sense of relief, knowing you are about to be free of military life and all its restrictions. No more orders! No more moves! No more deployments! No more missed holidays, birthdays, or anniversaries! Finally, for once, you and your loved one can make your own choices about where to live, what to do, and how to spend your time. You can choose a career, take vacations, do whatever you want without worrying that the "needs of the military" will outweigh your own needs and plans.

You probably also feel tremendous pride, not only in your service member's accomplishments, but also in your own. Yes, they have received promotions and medals and letters commending their service, and they earned every one of those accolades. But even if you have not been very involved in their military career, you deserve your own small moment of recognition. Your devotion and support helped them accomplish their mission. Your ability to pick up the slack and take care of yourself and your household on your own as needed gave your service member the freedom to spend time away from home without worry. Your willingness to be flexible, adapt, and make the most of each duty station kept your marriage thriving even in difficult times.

In numerous small ways, you have supported your loved one, helping them succeed in their military career. In fact, most military retirement ceremonies acknowledge the whole family as well as the service member. The spouse receives a letter of recognition and thanks for their support and sacrifices. Children are often recognized as well. The whole family shares the journey and rewards together.

Now the whole family is starting a new chapter, and this means transitioning into the civilian world. You've been waiting for this for a long time, but now that it's almost here you are probably wondering what awaits you and how you will adapt. Leaving the military is exciting, but also intimidating. There are many decisions to make: where to work, where to live, and how to get started.

Change always creates stress, even change you are happy to make. No matter how much you are looking forward to leaving the military, it's normal to be unsure exactly how you feel. Your current lifestyle, while filled with military demands and frustrations, is also familiar and—in some ways—comfortable. Your service member has job security, a housing allowance, and good medical insurance. When you leave the military, you will have more choices, but you will also have more decisions and new responsibilities. Facing the unknown is bound to create a bit of apprehension.

The demands and rewards of military life forge strong bonds of community that have no equivalent in the civilian world. This is true for both you and your service member. The longer you have been in military life, the more you have become a part of it. Leaving it may fill you with a sense of sadness, emptiness, or even dread. You may be celebrating the end of your service member's career and looking forward to a new life and still feel an underlying sense of sadness. This is a common mixture of emotions for a military spouse in your position. You are grieving the loss of one life as you move toward a new one.

When the military community has been your place in the world, you may feel a loss of identity when you leave it behind. Because of common experiences, you could immediately relate to and connect with other military spouses. You shared a common identity. But now your service member is preparing to leave the military, and it feels like your identity is slipping away.

You may struggle with this loss of identity for a while after your service member leaves the military. The longer they were in, the deeper this identity has been a defining part of your life. It's natural to struggle with losing both your identity as a spouse and the support of the community at the same time. You may wonder whether you are still a part of the military community or not.

Your service member will likely experience a loss of identity too, and they may feel it very deeply, even if they are ready to be done with military life and they can't wait to become a civilian. Very often we don't know what we are losing or what we will miss when we leave military life until the leaving is done. Your service member may have a hard time coming to terms with this loss. Also be aware that some posttraumatic issues or remnants of combat stress may emerge after retirement. You and your spouse will need time to process your military life and your new one. This is a very common experience for military couples. If counseling helps you come to terms with your old life and the new one, don't hesitate to find someone to help you through.

It may take some time, but you will realize your status as a military spouse will never matter as much as your experiences in military life. You won't be living the same life anymore, but no one can ever take away what you learned and the strength you gained from it. It will always be part of who you are, coloring the way you look at life and how you live it. Your time as a military spouse will always be part of who you are, but not all of who you are.

Even though the military may have been a big part of your life for a while, it's not your only identity. You are also a spouse to the one you love, and a daughter or son to someone who loves you. You may be a parent. You may be a runner, crafter, or baker. You may be a volunteer, or manager, or administrative assistant, or any number of other titles.

These are also part of your identity and who you are and who you will become in the future.

Leaving the military is something that happens to the whole family, not only the service member. Be sure to include conversations with your children about what this transition means to them. Acknowledge that the entire family has made sacrifices for your service member's career and the military mission. Be careful not to minimize the importance of that mission in your eagerness to leave it. It may leave the family wondering what their sacrifices were for.

Children who have only ever known military life may need time to adjust to life outside the military, especially if they are still living with you. In some ways this is like any of your previous moves. Be sure everyone in the family is prepared for the transition.

If you're feeling happy and sad, excited and apprehensive, hopeful and overwhelmed, plus a few more conflicting emotions, then you are feeling the way most military spouses feel about leaving the military. It's a natural response to the big, exciting change that is coming. It will take time, and sometimes it will be hard. But one day you will look around and realize you are settled and content, enjoying your new life.

You have made wonderful friends in your time in the military, and some of them will remain your lifelong friends. They are the ones who don't require explanations about your life. They just know. You may choose to stay connected to the military community in other ways or you may not. Either way, you won't forget your military life, but you don't want to live in the past either.

Now that you and your service member can choose your own lifestyle, dream big about the life you want to live. Every day will take you further from military life and closer to your new goals. It will be worth it.

Thank you for your sacrifices!

Epilogue
A Letter to Myself

Dear Writer,

Here you are, still in military housing, with its white walls and cheap kitchen cabinets. The baby is over on her playmat, stretching and cooing as she wakes from her nap. Another house (that makes five we've lived in, I think?) and another baby (she's definitely number five), and you're still pushing along through this military life.

It has been a long journey. Sometimes, the young girl who fell in love with that boy from work feels like another person. She was definitely smaller and thinner. She was also insecure, a perfectionist, and an overachiever. She had a five-year plan for going to college and getting a job.

It's been a long time since you were allowed to have a five-year plan. Lately, even the one-year plans are fluid, accommodating orders, a new baby, and a promotion. You aren't that young girl anymore. You might still be an overachiever, but you have learned to value flexibility over perfection. You have grown in confidence with each new challenge you have conquered. You are someone entirely different, and I'm proud of who you have become!

When you look back at this military journey, you remember every exhausting move and the painful separation of every deployment. You remember the mundane moments too: when Dan would come home for lunch in cammies, when you got lost driving around base, or when the kids were so excited to visit Daddy's office. This life has been full of ups and downs, disappointments and surprises. It hasn't been easy. But it has been very full.

Sometimes, you can see the light of retirement at the end of the tunnel. Just a few more years to go! But between now and retirement, there is still another move, and countless days where you will be home alone with all the kids. There will be more days of feeling exhausted and defeated. The laundry never ends. The sink is always full of dishes. There is always more work to do and deadlines to meet.

Every time you have it figured out, the children enter another stage and everything changes. Or the military comes up with a new way to throw a wrench into the cogs of this household. Sometimes, you get tired of answering questions from other military spouses and girlfriends, without anyone ever reaching out to ask how you are doing. It feels like the military just takes and takes. Your husband has been willing to give this much of his life away, but sometimes you simply have no more time or energy to give. You don't know how to find the will to keep going.

On those days, you have to take a step back and remind yourself how amazing you are. You have done incredible feats. You are the woman who gave birth alone, while a hurricane whipped the trees outside the hospital. You are the one who learned to drive a stick-shift car in a foreign country, with three kids in car seats in the back seat. During deployment, you learned how to juggle kids and do everything with one hand. You moved a hundred-pound propane tank on your own (with the kids' red wagon) because you are a strong and creative mama. You packed your entire house into boxes in one week, then unpacked it in a few days, and nothing was broken. You stayed loyal and faithful to your husband, even when you went weeks or months without hearing from him. You learned how to navigate strange cities before GPS, fell in love before dating apps, and nurtured a long-distance relationship before cellphones. You are strong, you are patient, and you have persisted.

Through all those experiences, you have learned something again and again: love will help you do what is difficult. You love your husband, and you love your children. No matter what this life throws your way, you will keep pushing forward and fighting for them. Yes, sometimes it's frustrating. Yes, there are days when you are exhausted. But through all of those moments, love has kept you going. So you're not going to give up now.

If there's one thing military life has taught you, it is this: you are stronger than you know. Years ago, that teenage girl didn't know if she could handle military life. Now you can tell her not only did she handle it, she crushed it. She adapted, she challenged herself, and she never stopped learning or growing. Every small challenge you faced gave you strength to get through the next one. Over time, you learned to do the impossible. You even learned how to use your experiences to help and inspire others. You can be proud of how far you have come. And you can be proud of where you are going. That inner strength is going to carry you to retirement, one day at a time. After that, it is going to carry you to another house, another job, and a whole new set of challenges.

Life may never stop challenging you. There will always be good days and bad days, even when your military years are far behind you. But now you know you have what it takes to conquer surprises and disappointments. You have learned to pivot, choose a new direction, and still reach out to help those around you. Military life has been an interesting journey and a good teacher. You will never forget the lessons you have learned, the friends you have made, and the experiences that made you who you are. So even on the hardest days, hold your head high. You can do amazing things! I can't wait to see what's next!

Acknowledgments

This book would not be possible without the support of many people:

My husband, Daniel, who has always encouraged me to write and believed I had something worthwhile to say. Obviously, I would not be in this military spouse role if it were not for your two decades of military service. I thank you for your incredible strength and perseverance, and all the sacrifices you have made for me and for our family. Thank you for always believing in me, for turning my writing hobby into a real LLC, and for all those Saturday mornings when you took the kids out of the house so I could write a few more chapters in peace.

My military spouse friends. There are too many to list here, but over the years so many different people had a role in shaping me as a military spouse. To all the incredible women from Mamas and Munchkins in North Carolina, who were there for me in the early years of babies and deployments, I thank you for all the play dates, the laughter, the venting sessions, the wine, and the parenting hacks. To my friends in Spain, thank you for teaching me to be brave and try new things and for sharing a million cultural experiences with me. To my friends from California, you are the reason I started writing. I wanted to encourage you through your first deployments with kids as I navigated those deployments with you. Thank you for putting up with my busy bunch, and for all the time we shared planning events and motivated each other.

My Facebook deployment group, Handle Deployment Like a Boss! For years, you all have shared your biggest celebrations and toughest moments with me. Together, we have comforted each other, discussed resources, and figured out how to navigate military life in the modern world. I'm grateful for all I have learned from the younger generation, and I thank you for bringing out the best in me and trusting me to be your mentor.

Finally, my kids: Sophie, Danny, Alex, Mary, and Elizabeth. All your lives, you have been teaching me and forcing me to grow. This book is about us—the experiences we have shared, the challenges we faced when Dad was away, and the big moves we made together. Thank you for your energy, for your constant strength in this military life, and for your proud smiles when you declare, "My Mom is a writer!"

Printed in the USA
CPSIA information can be obtained
at www.ICGtesting.com
LVHW030828160923
758405LV00049B/1187